Searching for Hillbillys

AN ULSTERMAN IN THE APPALACHIANS

JAMES MCCLELLAND

Searching for Hillbillys
© Copyright 1994 Causeway Press

Published by
Causeway Press
9 Ebrington Terrace,
Londonderry,
BT47 1JS
Northern Ireland

Contents

Acknowledgements 4

Introduction 5

The Blue Ridge Mountains...7

Black Rock Overlook 13

Pickin' and a Grinnin' 21

The Bikers 35

The Great Smoky Mountains 41

The Capital of the Smokies...49

The Music of Appalachia 57

From the Appalachians to the World.....................................67

Gospel Country 79

An Appalachian Pioneer...87

Acknowledgements

To the BBC for permission to transfer the spoken word to the pages of this book.

To Frank Robinson for advice and research material on the country music sections.

To Mike and Gail Richards for their invitation to Appalachia and for their hospitality and kindness.

To the people of the Appalachians for their welcome and co-operation.

Introduction

In the past eight years my work with the BBC has taken me all over Ireland, to many beautiful parts of the English countryside, and to the splendid grandeur of Scotland. In tandem with that my work as the director of an independent video production company has taken me to several other parts of the world. Along the way I've met the most interesting and fascinating people, made a lot of new friends and seen and done things that otherwise I would never even have heard of.

In 1993 my friends Mike and Gail Richards, whom I'd met when working for the large American textile company, Fruit of the Loom, invited me to spend some time with them at their new home. They had just moved to a little town in the foothills of the Blue Ridge mountains of north Georgia, in the Appalachians. As Mike described it to me on the phone it sounded an idyllic spot and I couldn't wait to get my plane tickets.

Visiting the Blue Ridge mountains, and subsequently, the Great Smoky mountains turned out to be the trip of a lifetime; the fulfilment of a long time dream.

The Appalachian region is a veritable gold mine of stories, songs and its own unique mountain culture so, as always on trips like these, packed amongst my luggage was my portable tape recorder.

Along the way I met and talked to all sorts of people. Mayors, councillors, government officials, visitors and tourists were all happy to talk to me and extol the virtues of this wonderful part of the world. When I came back home I made five programmes on the Appalachians for BBC. The content of those programmes makes up the core of this book.

I hope you enjoy this Appalachian Journey as much as I did.

James McClelland
Londonderry
September 1994

one

The Blue Ridge Mountains

"On a mountain in Virginia
Stands a lonesome pine.
Just below is the cabin home
Of that little girl of mine.
Her name is June and very, very soon
She'll belong to me,
For I know she waiting there for me
'Neath that lone pine tree.

In the Blue Ridge mountains of Virginia
On the trail of the lonesome pine.
In the pale moonshine our hearts entwine.
Where she carved her name
And I carved mine.
O June, just like the mountains, I'm blue,
Like the pine, I am lonesome for you.
In the Blue Ridge mountains of Virginia
On the trail of the lonesome pine."

T hose lines from the 1937 Laurel and Hardy film, *"Way Out West,"* sprung immediately to mind as I stood gazing over the scene before me. Like the guy in the song I also met, and fell in love with, a girl named June. So, when a record of that musical track from the movie was released a few years ago, I bought a copy and played it over and over again.

Each time I listened to it the romantic image of those Blue Ridge mountains increased my longing to see them for myself, some day. Now here I was, awe struck, in the midst of their splendid grandeur.

I had planned this trip for a long time and I'd dreamed of this moment for years - to stand on the '*holy ground*,' of the Appalachian Mountains.

The Appalachians - once Indian territory, then the place where my forefathers, the Scots-Irish, driven from their homeland by famine and persecution, came to start a new life - in the new world.

Those early settlers tamed its wilderness and ploughed its fields. From the Indians they learned to plant corn and to build log cabins. They got their first taste of such things as wild turkey and grits. And when the day's work was over they whiled away the long evenings making music on those fiddles, packed along with the few belongings brought with them from the old country. No wonder the Appalachians became the spawning ground for the bluegrass and country music that's so popular all over the world today.

A BAG OF M. & M.'S

At a tourist look-out point in North Georgia, Christopher Leeper, another Scots-Irish descendent, from Washington D.C, stood with me and together we surveyed the breathtaking scene.

"Isn't it a wonderful blessing to have eyes to see all this," I said to Christopher. *"Yes,"* he said, *"and not to be colour blind. If that was all monochromatic it would still be mighty beautiful, but having all the colours of the rainbow available to see it with the eye, is great."*

Christopher and I gazed at the view over a low sweeping valley. Away in the distance, some thirty or forty miles from where we stood, the sky met the trees. It was autumn, '*fall*' as the Americans call it, and the whole vista before us was one multicoloured splash of beauty. Gold, amber, russet and blue mingled with bright flaming red, fiery orange and the last traces of summer green. I could have looked until I'd looked my eyes away and still have longed for more. Christopher Leeper described it vividly.

"Right here you're looking across the states of Georgia, North Carolina and South Carolina. These are the Blue Ridge mountains of North Georgia and this is where they sort of peter out and become the Piedmont. The Blue Ridge mountains are not like the Rockies which are high and tough, even harsh. These mountains are soft. They're very soft and compelling, and they welcome you into their bosom."

"Just now as we look over this scene it's just as if somebody had scattered a huge bag of M.&M's across the mountains, with all the colours glinting in the evening sun. It's very quiet. The shadows are long and the angle of the sun, now at evening time, really makes the colours come alive. This is a great time of day."

"The blue mist in the distance is a part of this countryside. It's here all the time, hence the name Blue Ridge Mountains. Yes, it's very soft and beautiful - very, very beautiful - peaceful - thought provoking."

CAMPING

Christopher and his friends were camping down in the valley that lay below us. Somewhere through the leaves lay the Sumpter National Park, and through it rushes the Chitooga river, a glorious stretch of gushing, white water that's a favourite for canoeists and rafters. For him and his friends this was a sort of annual pilgrimage to photograph the autumn colours. Beside where we stood chatting, a very expensive camera stood on a sturdy tripod. It was pointing down the valley, capturing the scene our eyes feasted on. We stood for a while discussing photography - the film he used, shutter speeds, apertures, filters and then he told me about the excitement of camping in a place like this.

"Well it's something of an experience! The croaking of the tree frogs at night; the breeze blowing through the needles in the pines, and the rushing of the water in the distant river are the only sounds that disturb the silence of the place."

"And no more fear of being scalped," I added, alluding to the fact that this had once been Indian territory. *"No! No more fear of being scalped,"* he agreed. *"And in a way that's unfortunate. Not that it's less exciting because there's no more fear of being scalped, but that the Indians are no longer here. After all, they were here first."*

9

As I left Christopher Leeper his description of the scene came to me again. *"It's just as if somebody had scattered a huge bag of M.&M's across the mountains, with all the colours glinting in the evening sun."* I suggested he should be a copy-writer for the local tourist board. He'd have the crowds coming to this beautiful part of the world in even greater droves.

AUTUMN ATTRACTION

The tourists come, in multitudes, to the whole Appalachian region at this time every year. The autumn colours are a compelling attraction and the roads are choked with cars, packed with awe stricken passengers, from states for miles around. I saw registration plates from Tennessee, Arkansas, Florida, Pennsylvania, New York, North and South Carolina and Alabama, as well as hundreds from the state we were in, Georgia.

The topography of the region, with its rolling hills, long lush valleys and steep ravines, means that panoramic views meet the eye at every bend in the road. So beautiful is the area that the sound of the chirping of the crickets is almost swamped by the clicking of camera shutters. Mr Kodak must love the Appalachians!

I stayed with my friend Mike Richards and his wife Gail. They were splendid hosts, showering me with the kind of Southern hospitality and kindness for which the area is renowned. Wherever I wanted to go they took me; whatever I wanted to do they made sure I got to do it - and with style. Mike's mother, *"Mama"* Richards - all American grannies are called *"Mama"* - cooked real Southern fried chicken, with biscuits and gravy, and we ate until we sighed with satisfaction.

Mike and Gail had just moved to Rabun Gap, in the foothills of the Blue Ridge Mountains, a few months earlier. They hadn't settled on a permanent home and so, until they found the right place, were living in a house that belonged to the local town mayor. The mayor, in turn, was living nearby, looking after her mother, who was ill.

It was a cute house, built of timber and not much to look at from the outside. But once inside I was charmed by its all American feel.

The whole interior was open plan, except for a couple of small areas partitioned off for bedrooms and bathroom. In the living and kitchen area the ceiling went right up to the ridge of the house, giving a great sense of space. It was furnished with a table and chairs and a couple of large, soft sofas. Its polished wooden floor was scattered with rugs. Over against the wall a fat bellied, black, wood-burning stove stood sentinel and poked its long slender chimney up through the roof. Beside it, a stack of wood blocks stood in readiness for the cold winter nights that would soon set in.

The walls were hung with all manner of old fashioned farm implements, giving it a rustic, friendly feel, and there were plenty of pictures, mostly American rural scenes, to add warmth and colour.

One corner of this large, open plan room was the kitchen, with a long breakfast bar and high stools on which we sat drinking coffee, sometimes till the wee small hours.

Beside it, with a large, round teak table and chairs, was the dining area proper. Night by night that table groaned under the weight of southern home cooking. Mike and his family like to eat well. They like their guests to enjoy the best of hospitality too. I certainly didn't leave the Richard's home thinner than when I'd arrived there. But I'm not complaining!

Above the bedrooms another large open area was reached by a pine railed staircase. This was where I slept, in a large, comfortable bed, just below the window where the morning light streamed in between the chinks in the curtains.

From the living area two large patio doors opened out onto a grand veranda. I arrived at the Richard's home late at night, well after dark, and so didn't get my first view from that veranda until next morning. What a splendid surprise awaited me!

That first morning was bright and warm, even in late autumn, and the view up towards the mountains can only be described as a feast of beauty. I'm sure my mouth fell open in wonder at the sight. The autumn foliage was at its peak. A rich tapestry of colour stretched from where I stood, as far as the eye could see, some fifteen or twenty miles away. To say I was gob smacked sounds like an exaggeration - but I was.

On that same veranda we sat in the pleasantly cool evenings, after dinner, drinking coffee and chewing the fat. A beautiful stillness always seemed to pervade the evening air. Well almost a stillness. There was just enough wind to muster a gentle rustle in the crisp autumn leaves; just enough to send the odd handful of them fluttering to the ground to add to the autumn carpet of colour.

The myriad stars looked down from their peep-holes in the sky and the pale moon cast soft shadows all about us. Away in the distance the intermittent bark of a lone dog broke the silence, reminding us that, although this was a lonely, remote spot, we were not, in fact, alone.

Every time I sat there, admiring the multi-coloured kaleidoscope of autumn colour and listening to the incessant chirp of the crickets, I felt uplifted and inspired, wishing it could last forever.

two

Black Rock Overlook

On Saturday morning Mike and Gail, along with Mama Richards, drove me the few miles to Black Rock overlook. Climbing up a narrow twisting road, through forests of trees, we eventually arrived at the overlook, three thousand, four hundred and forty-six feet above the town of Clayton, also in North Georgia.

It was a splendid morning in late October. The sun shone pleasantly on the scene before us. Birds sang in the trees above and around their roots squirrels searched for nuts to add to their winter store. Far off, in the undergrowth, those crickets maintained their constant, one note tune.

Anthony Lampross has one of the best jobs any man could have. He's the manager of Black Rock overlook park and visitor centre. As we sat outside on a giant stone, warmed by the morning sun, and gazed across the vista before us Anthony, a Georgia man, born and bred, and with a southern drawl that I suspect was laid on especially thick for me, waxed enthusiastic.

"These are the Blue Ridge mountains and today our view probably extends about forty miles. On an extremely clear day, when there's absolutely no haze, you can probably see about eighty miles, but this is still a real, real pretty day to be up here."

"This range is the easternmost section of the Appalachian Mountains. They start here in Georgia and extend on up through South Carolina, North

Carolina, across Virginia and end, peter out really, right in the very southern end of Pennsylvania. So it's a rather long range and is considered to be one of the major ranges of the Appalachian Mountains. As well as that, this is one of the prettiest mountain regions in the eastern United States."

"A lot of our visitors are from the state of Florida, and Florida, as most people know, is sunny and tropical but very flat. As people drive up from Florida these are the first really true mountains they hit. And so, from that point, for many of them it's quite an experience - and a pleasant one too."

AN ADVENTURE LAND

Well once Anthony starts talking he's difficult to stop. It seemed he just couldn't wait to tell me all about this place, to extol its every virtue.

"This is an interesting area. We have the wild and scenic Chitooga river, which is a gorgeous area of white water river, just to our east. We have, in the southern end of the county, about fifteen minutes from here, a one thousand foot gorge, the Tiloola gorge. And then the famous Appalachian trail, that's a two thousand mile long walk, starts not too far from here. It begins here in Georgia and goes all the way to the state of Maine - so that's a long walk to say the least."

Looking down through the gorge below us, thickly cropped with trees of every breed and hue, to the river and then away beyond, to the hills and mountains, it seemed the perfect place to stage one of those adventure, mystery movies. You know the kind of thing I mean. A group of city office workers head off for a few days into the wilderness only to come face to face with a crazed criminal who starts bumping them of, one by one. The sheriff has to go to their rescue and he needs a man like Anthony Lampross to guide him.

"Well it's funny you should say that because a popular American movie called "Deliverance," was filmed right here in this county. Burt Reynolds was the main star and it was filmed back in 1972 or '73. It was about a group of city people who came to ride these white water rapids for one last time before the river was dammed up for a hydro-electric project. On the way they ran into some ruffians and had some bad experiences, but of course it was just fiction."

NO *"ROOFIANS!"*

Anthony was at pains to assure me that the film *was* just fiction. He didn't want anyone to get the impression that *"roof-ians,"* as he called them, did actually wander at large through his beloved Blue Ridge mountains.

"We have very, very little crime in this area and what little crime does exist is usually local people getting into skirmishes with other local people. The folks that come in from out of town just to visit are safe. We have very few incidents that involve visitors."

I wondered if there was anything akin to the famous skirmishes between the legendary Hatfields and McCoys of West Virginia and Kentucky.

"That sort of thing does occur a little bit, from time to time, but nothing like what people who're not from here imagine. It's different - much less boisterous."

What about the bears, I wondered. There must be a certain amount of potential danger to a stranger like me wandering through the woods unprepared.

"Yes, we have bears here. We've had bears right here in the park, even in the last few days. The community you see right down in the valley is the town of Clayton. Just last Wednesday a black bear went right through the middle of town and it caused quite a sensation. We also have bears right here in the park, we even had some problems this morning with bears messing about in the garbage cans and throwing refuse over the ground. But generally they never bother people. They're just looking for a hand out or a meal; they're not interested in causing injury to anybody, although now and again we'll get somebody who's frightened by a bear."

COMMON SENSE

Was Anthony Lampross really telling me that I could wander through these woods and mountains quite safely, unmolested, without any fear from bears? I found that almost impossible to believe.

"Well, a little common sense goes a long way. We encourage people when they're out in bear country to be real, real careful and watch where they put their food."

15

"And," I interjected *"If they do see a bear, adopt a lot of common sense and run!"* I don't think Anthony actually caught the drift of my attempt at humour. Even as I chuckled at it myself, he continued without a glimmer of a smile.

"Well, usually you won't have that kind of problem, a bear doesn't normally chase you. Wild bears are afraid of people and will give them plenty of room. Occasionally you will get a bear that is accustomed to getting a hand out when he sees people and then what he starts doing is associating people with food. That's when you have problems. A wild bear is going to get out of your way before you even see him. So the chances of actually running into a bear, in all honesty, are rather slim."

A PLUMB JOB!

Well by this time I was suitably comforted and returned to the subject of Anthony's fantastic job - managing this enormous tourist attraction. I suggested to him that he must have one of the most enviable jobs in the country. He didn't seem hard to persuade.

"I like it; it's a good job, I wouldn't argue with that. But, like any other job, it has it's moments and I don't suppose there's any such thing as a perfect job. We get to deal with people a lot and you have to be a people person when you're a park ranger. If you don't like people you're not going to last very long because we deal with several hundred thousand visitors a year - and that's a lot of folks. But I enjoy that, I enjoy meeting the wide variety of new people who come here every year, and I also enjoy being outside in the woods and observing the wild life. It's not bad."

As I've already explained, the big attraction of the blue ridge mountains on the week-end I was there was the autumn colours of the trees. Anthony Lampross told me I couldn't have picked a better time to come and see the beauties of an American *"fall."* This was the best it had been for about five years and this was also the peak week-end. It pleased me that, at last, I was talking to a man who could explain why the trees gave us such a wonderful display of colour at this time of year.

"As you look across the mountains look at all the colours that you see. You're looking at reds, golds, yellows, oranges. All the colours that are in these leaves right now are always there throughout the summer. But normally you don't see them because they're covered up by all the green, the chlorophyll in

the leaves. Chlorophyll's the substance that keeps the trees alive and allows them to continue to flourish throughout the summer. As the trees start shutting down their chlorophyll production in the fall, when these cold nights and cool days start to arrive, the chlorophyll fades away and basically what you're left with are the underlying colours. Those are the colours you see right now."

"We have a lot of different colours that we can see and, of course, as these other colours start to fade away obviously the leaves will become brown and ultimately fall off the tree and then we're left with the barren look that we have here in the wintertime. But right now, during these few short weeks, between the end of the production of chlorophyll and the turning of brown that's obviously going to be right behind that, we have a glorious display of fall colour."

FAR SIGHTED VISION

It was thanks to the intervention of a far sighted federal government, back in the 1930's, that we were able to gaze at the marvellous display of colour that morning at Blackrock overlook. Up till that time the natural forests of the Appalachian mountain range were being quickly stripped away by the indiscriminate search for timber, *"lumber,"* as the Americans call it, for building. But the government closed down the lumber camps, allowing the tree forests to grow back to their original wild state. They declared the area, or large parts of it, a national park, set up tourist information centres, appointed rangers and wardens to look after it, and thus preserved for successive generations an area of outstanding natural beauty.

Of course, preserving the environment isn't an easy matter. Each generation faces its own new threat and even as I drove through the Appalachian mountains I could see evidence of the latest attack on the forests. At first I thought it was the dreaded acid rain, but on further enquiry I found out that it the work of a non-native insect, the tiny *"Balsam Wooly Adelgid."* But of course, there's always a more imminent and frightening threat to forestry. Just a few days after I spoke to Anthony Lamross, it became a reality, in California.

"Obviously we always have to worry about things like forest fires. But anytime we get a problem like that our crews try to hop in on it real quick, along with the assistance of the U.S. Forestry Service, and we try to knock down any wild fires just as quick as we can."

The raging fires that swept through California in the autumn of 1993 were started deliberately and maliciously. They caused damage and left scars that will take a whole generation, and more, to repair. The threat to human life and the destruction of property are tragedies of momentous proportions in themselves, but it would be sad to see an area of such outstanding beauty as the Appalachians destroyed by fire.

WILD LIFE

Forest fire not only disfigures the countryside and threatens human life, it destroys wild life too. As Anthony Lampross explained, in the Appalachians, there's wildlife in abundance.

"We've got a tremendous range of wildlife here, even though you don't always see it. Most of our wild life is shy, it stays out of the way of people. But just to give you an idea of what you might expect to see in this area let me run through a few of them."

"We have three or four different species of hawks. Then we have owls and eagles. Eagles are a little bit rare, although both bald and golden eagles are occasionally spotted right here in these hills. We have a lot of mammals too, ranging from white tailed deer to the bears we talked about earlier. And we have a lot of small mammals too, like squirrels, chipmunks, foxes, cotton tail rabbits and other furry creatures."

"Because this area is so rich in wild life we have park naturalists that are assigned here during the summertime. There are a wide variety of programmes where people can sign up to go for a walk on various nature trails and hacking trails. On those walking trails we talk a little bit about the wild life, about the plant and animal life and also a little bit about the history of the Indians in this area. Through this the visitors get a little bit better idea of what this entire region is about and we've found that these programmes are rather popular."

"But we're not limited just to hikes. We do arts and crafts programmes for children. We do slide presentations and things like that which better acquaint people with what they're seeing up here. You have to remember that a lot of people come to this region from other areas and all this is pretty foreign to them, so we're trying to make something that's unfamiliar a little bit more familiar to them."

INJUNS!

Now of course, as I mentioned earlier, this part of the world, the Appalachians, was once Indian territory. Indeed the small town of Clayton that lay in the flat land of the plain, far below us, grew up at the point where two Indian trails intersected. In course of time a trading post was set up and from that grew the town of Clayton.

In these parts the main Indian tribe was the Cherokee, a highly civilised and organised people. The Cherokee were, in fact, a nation in their own right and, unlike the Apache, they were not scalp hunters. On the contrary, according to Anthony Lampross, they were a very friendly race of people.

"The Indians were not savages in any way. They were quite sophisticated for native Americans, and that's particularly true of the Cherokee."

"The capital of the Cherokee nation was located here in Georgia at a place called Nuachota and a state historic site still exists at that location. The Cherokees developed their own supreme court and their own newspaper. They didn't live in tepees or wigwams, as is portrayed in so many movies, but in log cabins and lodges, much as the early settlers did."

"They were not in any way a warring people. They weren't looking for a fight, in fact just the very opposite. They were really good people and they felt that the best way to get along with the pioneers that were entering this area was to make friends with them and adopt certain portions of their life style."

THE SCOTS IRISH

Anthony Lampross is himself twenty five per cent of Greek extraction and seventy five percent Scots-Irish. In Appalachia, as he pointed out, quite proudly, the Scots-Irish are everywhere.

"This entire region in the southern Appalachians is densely populated with people of Scots-Irish extraction. Obviously, now that you have people coming in from other places, the Scots-Irish influence is being somewhat watered down with people from elsewhere, but they're still the local Smoky mountain and Blue Ridge mountain people."

Is was the Scots-Irish who made this region what is was in early pioneer days. I suppose it would be no stretch of the truth to say that they also made it what it is today.

It was the settlers from Ulster and Scotland who came to this area in thousands, especially at the times of famine and religious persecution. They left behind only the soil and the memories of their homeland - everything else they brought with them. Their skills and talents; their determination and fortitude; their religion and faith, not packed in wooden trunks but tucked away in the secrecy of their stout hearts, came with them in their journey across the Atlantic to their new home in Appalachia.

And the legacy of their impact on the region can still be witnessed to this day. Small churches dot the landscape, evidence of their religious fervour. Well stocked farms, with acres of rich pastureland, testify to their industry and Presbyterian work ethic. And even today, the simplicity of their mountain dwellings, solid, functional and unornamented, is evidence of their contempt for outward show.

Even today the people of the Appalachians are warm hearted, friendly and hospitable to strangers. Wherever I went I was met with kindness, civility and co-operation. Individuals were willing, even glad to talk to me, but also anxious to hear about Ireland and to try to understand the problems of home.

Anthony Lampross believes that the Scots-Irish settled the Appalachian area well. When I asked him for his opinion of the people there was a definite pause in his racy patter, a prolonged silence as he moulded the words in his head and then a wry smile as he spoke.

"Well on this matter my opinion might be somewhat subjective, since I'm from that same stock, but I think they did a pretty good job. They were very, very independent people and really good about taking the natural resources they found here and making them work to their benefit. They were also extremely strong and determined folk. I have to say I'm real proud to be descended from them."

As I continued my journey through this wonderful Appalachian region I met many more unique local characters like Anthony Lampross. Their friendliness charmed me; their language and accents intrigued me, their simplicity of life humbled me, but perhaps most of all, their countryside astounded me.

three

Pickin' and a Grinnin'

"Run, run, run, run. Are we tooned up .....?"

The muffled voice struggles out through the cheap P.A. system, testing it's quality and quantity. In the background a bluegrass tune is picked on a badly tuned banjo. After a few bars the musical din is added to when a guitar and an autoharp join in.

It's Saturday night in Franklin, North Carolina. Since it's the last week of October it's already dark and there's a slight chill to the evening air, but that doesn't deter the crowd of two or three hundred who have gathered for what turns out to be a homespun jamboree. The punters sit around on deck chairs and stools sipping cups of hot coffee or soup, served from the only shop that's open, a small delicatessen, just behind the raised, covered stage in the centre of the town square.

On stage, the Georgia Mountain Boys, a bluegrass band from just over the state line, about ten miles away, entertain the crowd with their own brand of mountain music. The lead singer regales the crowd with a song about one of the most popular themes in country music.

"There's a fast train at the station
  Waiting to carry me home.
When the sun comes up in the mornin'
  I'll be on that train and gone.
O what a happy reunion
  When I step out of the door.
And the pure, sweet dreams
  Of the mountain and streams
Have all come true once more."

PICKIN' ON THE SQUARE

The music is hardly up to Nashville standards, but then the audience isn't paying Nashville prices. This is a free concert, held every Saturday night from mid May till the end of October. It entertains strangers like me and brings the towns-people and the country folks together. "Pickin' on the Square" they call it, and it's just good ole, down home music and fun.

"And the sweet, sweet dreams
  Of the mountain and streams
Have all come true once more."

The song ends and the crowd applauds politely. What sounds like sighs of relief expel from the lungs of the singer, as if to say *"Thank goodness I made it to the end of that one."*

Another figure steps forward to the microphone. He's a tall, somewhat rounded, imposing character, who turns out to be Ed Henson, the mayor of this sleepy little mountain town.

"MOONSHINE"

The band has only played about two songs but Ed announces that the fellas are going to take a break now - it's time for drink. There isn't a can of beer in sight but Ed proceeds to tell a joke about illicit liquor - *"moonshine,"* as it's called in these parts. Ed doesn't speak with a typical southern drawl but rather, spits out the words in one long continuous stream.

"This old white mountain liquor they make here in the mountains, they should call it summer vacation, because two drinks of it and school's out!"

The quip gets the kind of laughter that comes from people who've heard it all before, but Ed proceeds, with another joke in the same vein.

"There was these three guys sitting round the camp fire some time back and drinking some of this stuff. Then one of them had to get up and walk off for a minute. Do you know it took the other two fifteen minutes to realise which one of them wasn't there!"

Ed, who's the sort of unofficial master of ceremonies for the night, tells a few more stories and then introduces the next artist; an aged local lady who plays square dance music on the fiddle in a style that can most kindly be described as - novel. She scratches out tune after tune to the accompaniment of a guitar player who sometimes knows exactly which chords to play - and sometimes doesn't!

The locals eye me suspiciously, my head wrapped in headphones, my hands clutching a microphone as I wander through the crowd in search of the best sounds. Some of them ask me what I'm doing and when I tell them, their interest is suddenly transferred to my Irish accent, which they invariably think is English. When I tell them where I'm from their eyes light up and they stand six inches taller as they boast of their Scots-Irish ancestry.

LADY IN BLACK

Then I spot the strange figure of a woman moving swiftly through the crowd. She's dressed all in black, she's hung with strings of pearls, and she's swishing a large feather and causing great excitement in the crowd, especially amongst the men. Eventually, we come face to face.

"What are you up to?" I enquire politely enough.

"Anything! You name it, I'm up to it!" She replies with a cheeky charm and the most attractive Scarlet O'Hara accent.

I enquire further, hoping this time for a more serious and detailed response *"Well what are you doing here?"*

"Oh I come every year about a week before Halloween. I dress all up because at Halloween I'm a wicked witch - I'm really the good witch of Western North Carolina - and I love to come to the Pickin' on the Square. I don't think I'm dressed appropriately, do you?

I suggested that her outfit would have been better suited to someone about to dance the Charleston. She agreed.

"Exactly! I'm leaving for Charleston immediately after this performance tonight."

She was lying, of course, or pulling my leg. So what was she really up to? I was to find that out later, for, as quickly as she came she was gone, back into the gloom of the night to torture and torment more male hearts. However, she promised to meet me later.

BURL IVES?

Earlier, back stage, I'd bumped into a figure who looked for all the world like Burl Ives. He had that same rotund belly, that same round, bearded face, and the guitar hung over his shoulder by a broad strap completed the picture. When I commented on the likeness he mumbled,

"Burl Ives taught me the first chords I ever played on the git-ar."

He turned out to be Bill Myers and he claimed to have once played with *"The Sons of the Pioneers,"* a country group founded by Roy Rogers, back in the thirties. I don't know if he ever did but now he's on stage with his very much younger, peroxide blonde wife, who vamps on the harmonica, as he strums guitar and sings a song about another train.

"Well I'm leavin' on that Bryson city trainnnn ......
Leavin' on that Smoky Mountain trainnnn .....
Well this same old train that brought me here
And it's gonna take me back againnnn ...

"Oh my darlin' you can't love three ...
Oh my darlin' you can't love three ..
Well you can't love three and still love me
Oh my darlin' you can't love three."

The blond wife persistently vamps away on the harmonica as Bill Myers sings another verse of the song, exactly the same as the last one, except that *"Oh my darlin' you can't love three,"* is substituted by *"Oh my darlin' you can't love four."*

As Bill goes back to the chorus *"I'm leavin' on that Smoky Mountain train,"* I wander off into the night for my promised rendezvous with that strangely clad lady I'd met earlier.

THE WICKED WITCH!

I finally caught up with her in a more secluded spot, away from the blast of the loudspeakers. I had yet to discover her name and when I asked her she announced it in that immaculate Scarlet O'Hara accent.

"My name is Patti McClure. I taught school for twenty-eight years and I'm also a story teller. I've gone all over the place telling my stories. I was the first story teller on the SS. Norway Cruise line, with Mickey Gilley, Ralf Emery and George Jones, in 1989. I'm also the good witch of Western North Carolina. On Halloween I turn into a real authentic looking witch and I go all around," - she adopts an evil, frightening accent - *"and I talk like a real witch and I try to get someone to ride on my broom and I tell stories everywhere for Halloween."*

Patti McClure is from eastern North Carolina but has lived in Franklin for the past fourteen years. I'm transfixed by her impeccable use of the language, with every word perfectly enunciated.

"People tell me I talk funny and I tell them, 'Yes!' But I speak grammatically correctly. I'm a fanatic about English and how people do speak."

Patti learns that I'm from Ireland and at the news her eyes light up and she becomes even more excited. She's never been to the Emerald Isle but that doesn't stop her talking about it like a native.

"I love Ireland and I love all of the Irish sayings. I copy them because I'm also a poet and I use them in my poems about birthdays, weddings, retirements and anything else that's going on."

The Scots-Irish are wonderful people. They are very giving and very caring. I just love people from Ireland and I wish that I could go to Ireland. In fact, I was going this Christmas to England and Ireland but all that came to a halt because of my heart problems."

THE BEEPER

Around Patti's neck there's a long chain and hanging on the end of it, at about waist level, there's a small plastic box. She'd told me earlier this was her heart beeper. I didn't believe her, but now she explains.

"I have had three massive heart attacks and I only have twenty per cent of my heart functioning. "

I suggest to her that if she's this energetic and exuberant with only twenty per cent of her heart working properly, she'd be a danger to the world if she had all her heart. It seems, however, my idea wasn't original.

"That's what everybody says. No one can believe how much energy I have, not even the doctors. However I do get tired, especially walking up inclines and steps.

Whether it's the evening light, the black outfit she's wearing or the judicious application of make up but, to me, Patti McClure looks the very picture of health. She lifts her eyes heavenward.

"God has been so good to me. God has taken every step of the way with me. I am a Christian and I believe that he has never not answered a prayer for me. I am a walking miracle! I had heart failure and was gone for a minute and a half. I have two sons. One is twenty and the other is twenty-three and they were standing outside the door when the doctors said 'Miss Patti has passed away. There's no heart-beat.'

"So they shocked me and a lady in the emergency room said 'Dear God please don't take Miss Patti now, she has so much to do.' "Well my heart started beating again and I have spent since 1989 going around and telling people how good God has been to me and trying to make other people happy. And I am going to go and do that until I drop dead."

Meanwhile, Patti is waiting for that beeper to go off.

"When this beeper goes off I go to the telephone and I call the Medical Centre in Charlotte, North Carolina and they will say 'Miss Patti, we have a

heart for you.' *"They will either tell me to go to Angel Hospital and they will send a helicopter for me, or they might tell me to drive to Ashville where there'll be a Lear Jet waiting to take me. But they have all of that planned."*

"When they find the heart it might be a thousand miles away and it only lasts for four hours, so I have to get to the hospital in time to get that heart. And if I get a new heart - they had better look out!"

To me, walking about through life every day, waiting for a little plastic box hung about your neck to sound it's alert, is a rather cheerless prospect. Patti McClure, however, is a unique individual; one of the most remarkable people I've ever had the good fortune to meet.

"I'm very excited! I think that this is what God wants me to do. I'm gonna be a heart transplant candidate that lives to tell what a wonderful thing all of this is. I'm also devoting a lot of my time and effort into trying to encourage people to be organ donors. You know we don't need our organs when we die. We don't need them on earth and we don't need them in heaven. But people need them. One person that will donate the body parts can be life for seven other people. "

FUNNY GIRL

Sobering and worthwhile words from Patti McClure. However, Patti isn't just a story teller, a poet and something of an actress, she has a fund of jokes too, including a few that are none too complimentary of America's first citizen. And she assured me that she has been a life long Democrat. Her vote helped to put Bill Clinton in the White House, but you wouldn't think so when you listen to her jokes.

"Bill Clinton is probably not the most popular president we've ever had but I suppose it's a kind of a sign that you've arrived when people tell jokes about you.

"These two little boys were sitting on the river bank and they were fishing. They had been there quite a while when Bill Clinton came by in a great big fishing boat which was skimming over the waves, quite fast. All of a sudden the boat made a very quick turn and Mr. Clinton was thrown completely off balance."

In Patti McClure's joke Bill Clinton can't swim and so, there he is, floundering in the water and about to go down for the third time. His screams for help attracted the attention of the two young anglers.

"They looked at each other and decided they'd have to do something. So they dived in the water, swam to where Bill Clinton was gasping his last, dragged him to the bank, and hauled him out of the water."

Drawing on their boy scout skills the heroes applied artificial respiration to the dying president and, just in the nick of time, managed to revive him. After splurting out what seemed like gallons of muddy river water, Mr. Clinton sat up, blurted his thanks to the boys and asked *"Do you know who I am."*

"No Sir, we don't, the boys confessed. The great man introduced himself. 'Well I'm Bill Clinton and I'm the president of the United States of America. The boys looked at him in stunned silence as he continued. 'Boys, for saving my life you both can have any wish you want.

"He turned to the first little boy and asked 'What can I do for you son. What would you like?'

The first little boy knew an opportunity when he saw one. He must have realised the magnitude of his heroic deed and he was determined to capitalise on it. Without a pause for breath he blurted out.

"Well Sir, times have been hard for me and my family and my Daddy hasn't worked in years. I wish you'd give him a job in the White House so he can make lots of money and we could have a nice house and he could buy us all the things we need."

"Without hesitation, Bill Clinton said 'As soon as I can get cleaned up and get back to my office your daddy will have a job, I promise."

The second little boy observes all this with a certain degree of unbelief. Bill Clinton asks him what he wants in return for helping to save his life. The lad stammers his answer.

"Eh, I believe I would like a grave in the Arlington cemetery, Mr. President. The great man is taken aback by this strange request from one so young. 'You want a grave in the Arlington cemetery! Why a child like you should want

something far more exciting than that. You should be asking for a toy, a computer game, something far more wonderful that a grave in the Arlington cemetery."

The boy shook his head and replied *"No Sir, that's what I want."*

The President, still mystified by the unexpected nature of the boy's request just had to ask him why a grave in the Arlington cemetery was all he wanted. In her rapid fire style Patti McClure delivers the punch line with relish.

"Well Sir, when I goes home and tells my Daddy I saved the President's life - he's gonna kill me!"

I say good-bye to Patti McClure and make my way back to the bandstand here the fiddles are still hummin' and the guitars still strummin'.

THE OLD TIME RELIGION

A couple of young people give an exhibition of clog dancing, something I didn't know was a feature of Appalachian culture. It takes a lot of skill, it makes a lot of noise, and it consumes a lot of energy. I suppose it's for this reason that, apart from the couple who demonstrate the dance, the only ones who last the distance are the few children who join in the fun.

The evening wears on, and now the band is playing a selection of the old gospel favourites, as if, I suppose, to draw a sanctifying veil over the night's proceedings. These are mountain folk, mainly of Protestant Scots/Irish stock, and the old time religion still runs deep in their blood. Songs about *"Mama,"* the old homestead, and heaven, strike the right chord in their hearts.

"Amazing grace, how sweet the sound,
*   That saved a wretch like me.*
I once was lost but now am found,
*   Was blind but now I see."*

MR. MAYOR

Ed Henson, the mayor and M.C. for tonight's *"Pickin' on the Square,'* hovers around the band stand for most of the night. In between organising the acts as they go on stage, he dishes out coffee to the players, greets visitors like me and keeps a watchful eye on the entire proceedings.

"Pickin on the square begins about the middle of May and goes on right through to about the end of October.

"Each Saturday night we have what we call a house band, and tonight our house band was 'The Georgia Mountain Boys,' from down in Georgia. We live in the South Western part of North Carolina, which is near Georgia, Tennessee and South Carolina and these guys are about the best in Bluegrass in this area.

"Even though it was a little cold tonight we had a good crowd and everybody seemed to be having a good time and I noticed, James, that you too looked like you were having a good time and so we're glad that you were enjoying yourself."

There was no insincerity in my thanks to him. I really had enjoyed the evening. It had been a memorable experience - like a bit of old Appalachia brought to life for the night. But why would a little town, in such a remote mountain area, take the trouble to host an event like this every Saturday night throughout the summer? Ed Henson had the answer.

"One reason for the Saturday night 'Pickin' on the Square,' is to preserve this traditional old mountain music. It's been around this area for a very long time, hundreds of years in fact, and we don't want it to die out - to be forgotten.

"As well as that, on nights like this, we close off several streets around the square and keep out the traffic. This means that our children can have the freedom to move around and enjoy themselves. There's no lack of security here; it's a very safe place, and we can all meet just to see family and friends. Our children can come out too, and be free to roam around and be perfectly safe in doing so."

THE MOUNTAIN MAN

Listening in to most of this conversation was a most unusual character - well at least he was unusually dressed! He was clad in well worn, old fashioned bib and brace overalls - the type worn by carpenters years ago.

What struck me was that hardly any of the original blue denim was visible because gaily coloured patches had been sewn all over the cloth. The patches were the kind of thing my granny used years ago to make patch-work quilts, and they gave the tall, lean wearer a kind of upmarket scarecrow appearance.

He stepped forward as Ed Henson introduced him.

"This is Andrew Parker, one of the members of the Smoky Mountain Boys."

Andrew drawled a genial *"Howdy do!"*

He was as genial as his greeting. His bronze, well lived in face sported a pair of twinkling eyes that bespoke the mischief that would surface later. As I looked him up and down I quickly realised that, at last, I was face to face with a true mountain man.

I could imagine him following a team of horses, ploughing a single furrow in black dirt earth. Or on the side of a hill, felling timber to build a log cabin. Or sitting on the porch of that same log cabin, pickin' tunes on his guitar on a cool summer evening.

APPALACHIAN TO THE CORE

For me, Andrew Parker epitomised the Appalachian people. Straight in his talk as he was in his six foot tall frame. Honest as the day is long, and dependable as the very hills in which he lived.

Even though he was a good few years my senior he persistently addressed me as *"Sir,"* a mark of respect reserved usually for elders, but also afforded to welcome guests.

His answers to my questions were brief, clipped and to the point.

"I'm no the leader of the group. Ed Teague's the leader but I do most of the singin', me and Lawton does, and we really enjoy what we do."

"You seem to do most of the joke telling too."

"Yes I do."

"And some of those jokes are none too complimentary about your president, Bill Clinton."

"Yes that's right," he chuckles.

"Would that indicate a certain political persuasion in these parts," I enquired.

"Aw, probably so! The chuckles last longer.

You'll say no more than that."

"Am, I'd better not say no more than that."

"Is this the point where you plead the fifth amendment?"

"Yes Sir, I believe so!"

BLUEGRASS GOSPEL

Andrew Parker and his friends have been playing together, as a group, for about five years but their love of Bluegrass goes back a lot longer.

"We've been playing all of our lives. I played gospel music for all my life, I guess, just about. Me and Ed was raised up together, he's a little bit older than me, but we were raised right down clear across the line on the edge of Georgia. Of course we got separated, hadn't seen each other in years, and we just happened to run up together at a place one night and started getting together and that's where we came up with the idea of the Georgia Mountain Boys.

During tonight's *"Pickin' on the Square,"* Andrew and his friends had played a few gospel numbers, so when he mentioned that he'd been playing gospel all his life, my ears pricked up.

" I was raised in a Christian family; raised to go to church, and I just love gospel music - it's important to me.

"So," I asked, *"Are you a good livin' American boy then?"*

"Yes Sir, I think so. A lot of people might not agree but I think so."

THE BLUEGRASS BAND

Andrew follows the claim with another long chuckle. A few other bystanders who overhear us, join in the laughter. Perhaps they all know something that

I don't. I decide to move the conversation on by enquiring about the make up of a traditional Bluegrass band.

"Well, different Bluegrass bands has got different things and it all depends on what's available. If you notice we've got three guitars and a banjer (banjo). *Lots of Bluegrass bands has fiddles, mandolins, dobros and stuff like that, but we're not fortunate enough to have anybody who can play all of those instruments, so we just do the best we can with what we've got."*

"And what about those outlandish outfits," I wondered, *"reminiscent, in some respects, of the Beverley Hill Billys?*

"The outfits are not really important. We just come up, with these things and then people begin to expect them and look for them when you go back to where you've been before. Now if you notice my hat!

THE HAT

I had indeed noticed the hat, a black Napoleon type affair, strewn with those little metal badges that are sold everywhere in the world. I'm sure you know the kind of thing I mean - *"North Carolina Steam Engine Society"* - *"Smoky Mountain Nature Trails"* - *"Bluegrass is fun!"* The hat was barely visible beneath this mass of metal, and to top it all, there was a big sign on the front of the hat which proclaimed *"I'm not as dumb as you look!"* There was another large sign on the back.

"It says 'My weekend hat.' No matter what day of the week I wear it, it's on my weak end."

Again Andrew gave a long low chuckle and we said good-bye.

Franklin, North Carolina, will stay in my memory for a long time. Oh I know the music wasn't fantastic; there were plenty of bum notes, and the loud-speaker system left a lot to be desired. But none of that mattered. I was among warm, friendly, simple people - my own kin folk from the new world - and I felt at home with them. In the next few days I moved on from the Blue Ridge Mountains, to the Great Smokies, still in the Appalachians. In Gatlinburg, Tennessee they made me an honorary *"Gatlinburg Mountaineer,"* with a certificate to prove it, but for hospitality and homeliness the people of Franklin, North Carolina have got to be hard to beat.

four

The Bikers

The glories of Blackrock Overlook behind us, Mike and Gail drive me around the nearby region of the Blue Ridge mountains.

We end up in Franklin, the same place where the *"Pickin on the Square,"* was held. Driving through beautiful countryside and gulping in large lung fulls of fresh air is hungry work, so we stop at a quaint wayside eating place and sample some all American home cooking.

There's a bunch of leather jacketed guys eating at the same place, and I wonder about them. I make a comment on the wide brimmed, black hat worn by one lean faced young man. He invites me outside!

He's not a very big guy, but he looks mean and wiry. I don't know where he's from - but I do know I'm a stranger in these parts - and I've never been proved in a scrap. With more than a measure of trepidation I follow him.

Outside, on the street, there's about another thirty of these guys - and a few girls too. Gradually, I'm aware of a faint throbbing noise in the air. It gets louder, indicating that the source is getting closer. The throbbing increases to a crescendo and I spin round searching for clues to its origin. Suddenly, it appears and my heart lifts. Roaring past us goes a gleaming, monstrous, vibrant, chrome and black beast - a motorcycle. But this is not just any old motorcycle - this is one of the most exclusive two-wheeled mounts in the world - a Harley Davidson.

HARLEY MEN

The young man in the fancy black hat turns out to be Michael, from Florida. He, and all the other *"Harley"* men who have invaded Franklin this sunny afternoon, are here for their own personal tour of the splendours of an American fall. Michael turns out to be a very courteous and helpful young man and he seems quite flattered that a stranger from so far away should show an interest in a passing motorcycle gang.

"We've got twenty-eight people here with us on this trip and we're just up here in the mountains looking at some fall colours and enjoying the roads up here in North Carolina."

Michael's outfit catches my eye. It's not at all like the kind of thing worn by motor-bike riders in this country. Apart from the cowboy hat, he wears an expensive looking black shirt and a pair of blue denim jeans. Over the jeans, black leather chaps protect from the wind and dust and, on his feet, a pair of black, calf length boots, with high heels and silver studs, add to the cowboy image. A red, silk handkerchief, tied loosely around his neck, completes the picture.

"Today's a little cool and so we're dressed in several layers to keep warm. I also have a heavy leather jacket that I'll wear when I'm riding. The leather keeps the wind from cutting through and also, if anything serious were to happen, it protects you in the event of an unfortunate fall."

THE AMERICAN DREAM MACHINE

In this age when Japan has taken over the manufacture and supply of the best in everything I wondered why the passionate interest in a machine built in America. After all, almost every Grand Prix in the last couple of decades has been won by a rider on a Honda, a Yamaha, a Suzuki or a Kawasaki. Michael, however, remains faithful to his treasured marque.

"Actually Harley Davidson commands over sixty per cent of the American big bike market. In the big touring bikes they would control a bigger share of the market if they could only produce more. This year they'll produce eighty thousand bikes and their production is entirely sold out for the next twelve months."

He continues to enthuse over the Harley Davidson and to further ply me with facts and figures.

"The Harley Davidson today is a phenomenon that isn't going to go away. They've been around for a long time, in fact they've just celebrated their ninetieth birthday. They're the oldest American, indeed, the only American motor-cycle company still in existence. All over the world they're the most sought after machines on two wheels."

Harley Davidson riders are a breed apart. The bikes themselves are very expensive, so I wondered if Michael and his friends were wealthy lawyers or doctors. It turned out that my guess wasn't so far off the mark.

"We have doctors, lawyers and maybe even a few Indian chiefs here in this group. We're all professional, people and some of us own more than one bike. Some of us have wives and girl-friends who are also riding. In fact, this bike right here actually is my wife's, and she's a doctor."

The lady in question is standing only a few yards away and he calls her over. Her name is Karen and it turns out she's not just a doctor, she's a psychologist.

It was probably just my imagination but within the first few seconds of our meeting I couldn't help feeling that, even as we were being introduced, she was analysing me, and deciding that my interest in their Harley Davidson motor-cycle club was proof enough that I was just as crazy as they were. However, she was diplomatic enough not to tell me so.

For me, Karen epitomised the all American sixties girl. Like her husband, she too wore blue denim jeans with black leather chaps and cowboy boots. Her matching denim jacket, studded with imitation gemstones, had *"Harley Davidson,"* emblazoned across the back in large letters and she proudly twirled to show it off. Around her trim waist she had slung a money pouch and, as if to make sure that everyone knew she was a *"Harley"* fan, across the shiny peak of her natty black hat was printed *"Harley Davidson Motorcycles."*

MACHO IMAGE

These are big, heavy, macho man bikes so I wondered what a pretty lass like Karen was doing entangling herself in an outfit like this. I assumed a lot of it had to do with her husband's influence.

"I guess that's so. It's partly his business and I figure you have to go with the flow. So I learned how to ride a couple of years ago and it's challenging, but it's good for me."

I put to Karen my thoughts about *"Harleys,"* portraying something of a macho image, and not for dainty, feminine persons like herself. However, she dismissed the notion.

"Well I'm ridin' a big one and I'm doing the best I can to keep up. It was difficult to get my skills up at the beginning, but now that I've got those skills it's not so difficult."

I ventured to ask Karen if there was any possibility of a pillion ride on the back of her bike. She threw her head back, sending her long golden tresses flying in the air, and laughed at the idea.

"Oh, you wouldn't want to get on the back of my bike." She laughed convulsively and her husband joined in. *"It's not safe yet. Another couple of years and maybe I could take you for a ride, but not right now.* She laughed again.

HELL'S ANGELS?

The leader of this group of Hell's Angel look alikes was Todd, a burly solicitor, from Washington D.C. I stress the fact that they're just look alikes. Their behaviour, both on and off the road is exemplary. Anyway, back to Todd, the leader, whose surname I was never given, perhaps for legal reasons. Todd organised this whole trip; he does it every year, making contact with Harley owners from New England, in the north, to Florida, in the south.

"Well we have about eight states represented on this run and it's called "The Smoky Mountain Roundup." It's really a group of people that have been off-shore boat racing together for the past decade. Of late they've all sort of filtered over to Harley Davidsons and to motorcycle riding as a hobby and we decided to put a group together. They're mostly attorneys, doctors, business and professional people and every year around this time we have a three day rally. We're at a country club over in Maggie Valley, a lovely area in the Smoky Mountains, and each day we're touring different sections of this region to view the fall colours which this region is known for at this time of year.

Ah, it was those fall colours again! It seems the world and his wife wants to be in the mountains at this time of year.

NO CHICKEN

I suggested to Todd that, like myself, he was no youngster. I actually used a saying of my mother's *"You won't tear in the pluckin.'"* He understood. I put it to him that, at his time of life, he would be expected to be putting his feet up by the fire, calling for his pipe and slippers and contenting himself with just reading motorcycle magazines, rather than still riding the dangerous things.

"Well if you're insinuating that I'm long of tooth I don't think that description fits anybody here. We run in age anywhere from between forty to sixty-five years old. I mentioned to you earlier that we've all been active racers in the off-shore power boat circuit and that's a very vigorous sport, so if we can get out there and handle that I think we can handle a couple of two wheelers."

"But this is basically a social outing, taking everybody around to three different locations out of about twenty different tours that one could do in this region."

I've already referred to Todd and his travelling companions as *"Hell's Angel look alikes,"* so I wondered how the local police reacted to their presence on their patch.

"The police don't have any worries about a group such as ours. They're very pleased to see us, in fact. We're professional riders and ride in formation and they can spot immediately, by the manner of road etiquette that we practice, whether we're sophisticated riders or just a bunch of hacks. So we have no problems with the police at all."

Michael called me again. It was time for my ride on the back of a Harley. Donning a black leather jacket which he supplied, and squeezing my head into Karen's slightly small helmet, I prepared for the experience of a lifetime.

MOUNTING UP

The ride on the big Harley was even better than I'd expected. It was large, roomy you could say, and so comfortable. It was a beautiful day, and the high pillion seat gave me a panoramic view of the whole countryside. There were none of the restrictions you have in a car, no windows to steam up, no roof above to hinder the view of the sky - it was the ideal way to drink in the beauties of the Appalachian fall.

Beneath us the huge engine thudded reliably and sent its vibrations up through the seat and through my whole body. A few miles of this, I thought, would soon tone up the muscles of the thighs and buttocks.

Along country roads and through leafy glades Michael took me, the sun sparkling on the chrome handlebars, and the wind massaging a pink glow into my cheeks. When he cranked the bike over for a tight corner, I leaned with him, adding to the thrill of speed. But all the time I felt safe, assured, comfortable.

At the end of our short trip Michael pulled the big Harley to a gentle stop and the powerful engine reduced its vibrant thud to a gentle purr. My lungs had been refilled with fresh, clean air and my senses heightened by the experience on two wheels.

Sadly it was time for both them and me to leave Franklin and press on with the rest of our journeys. I watched them mount up and ride off into the distance, with one combined, deafening but beautiful roar - and how I wished I could have gone with them.

five

The Great Smoky Mountains

"T ake four forty one north, through Dillsboro, and then you continue on that to Cherokee, where there's an Indian reservation. There's quite a lot to see in Cherokee .... "

The guide in the Smoky Mountains visitor centre, near Franklin, North Carolina points out the best route to the splendours of the Great Smoky Mountains, more than fifty miles away.

Everybody has told me how fantastic the Smokies are and I can't wait to see them for myself. I gather up the brochures, check the map and buy a tape featuring Smoky Mountain gospel music. Nobody in the shop has heard the music but they've been told it's good. I wonder.

I'm being driven again today by Gail Richards, in her natty Ford convertible. Mama Richards is in the front beside Gail and I squeeze into the rather small back seat. However, for this trip, I'd be happy to ride on a buck-board. Gail revs up the engine, pops the cassette into the player and we set off. In a few minutes we're back on the open road, under blue skies, and with hardly another vehicle in sight. From the car stereo the most delightful strains of authentic Appalachian mountain music, played on hand crafted instruments and by local musicians, fills the air. It's beautiful! Gail and I hum along to the old familiar gospel favourites. Mama Richards taps her feet.

Following the guide's instructions we drive on up through the Blue Ridge mountains and into the Great Smokies.

Looking back on that journey now all I can say is that it was absolutely fabulous. No words of mine are adequate to describe the unparalleled beauty of the place. At every bend in the road I was stunned by yet another majestic vista that outshone the one before.

A GRANDSTAND VIEW

At one of the mountain lay byes, when we pulled in to take still more pictures of the stunning scenery, Gail rolled back the canvas hood. Now we had an open top car. From my slightly elevated back seat I had a grandstand view of the unfolding panorama. We drove beneath sky-scraper high canopies of golden trees, all the more spectacular against the blue sky that peeped through the gaps in the leaves.

Near the top of the mountain climb we stopped for petrol. Inside the gas station they served constantly fresh coffee. I grabbed a cup and stood outside sipping it slowly. It was late morning, and the clean mountain air filling my lungs was like a tonic; the beauty of the hills and mountains about me, with their never ending profusion of colour, like a therapy.

A little further on we came to Cherokee, a small town in a kind of clearing in the mountains. Its wide streets and modern shops can't conceal the fact that Indians have lived there for centuries, for everywhere you look there are stores displaying all manner of Indian goods. Genuine rugs, wall hangings, beads and necklaces, carvings, shawls, miniature totem poles and a thousand other trinkets invite the tourist to take home a little bit of Cherokee history with them.

INJUNS!

There's still an Indian reservation in Cherokee, in fact there are six communities in all. They have great Indian names too, Yellowhill, Birdtown, Painttown, Snowbird, Big Cove and Wolftown. And there are a multitude of Cherokee attractions. There's a visitor centre, two museums, one on the history of the American Indian, the other on the history of the Cherokee.

There's a wax museum, a model Indian village and an arts and crafts centre. There's even a couple of places where you can play Indian bingo, although how it differs from ordinary bingo I never found out.

Long before Columbus discovered the "New World," or Spanish explorer Hernando deSoto first set foot in the Great Smoky Mountains, in 1540, the Cherokee territory stretched from the Ohio river to the north, and southward into Georgia and Alabama.

Here, twenty-five thousand Cherokees ruled over 135,000 square miles covering parts of what are now eight states. Their vast territorial holdings were only surpassed by the depth of their culture and heritage, dating back unnumbered generations.

Their land holdings have long since disappeared, but today a strong pride keeps the past alive through renewed interest in legends, stories, myths, language and the crafts of their ancestors.

LEGEND AND TRADITION

Cherokee legend, for example, explains that the Great Smoky Mountains were created by a Great Buzzard. When the earth was soft and still forming the Great Buzzard flew too close and as it wing tips pushed the ground down, the mountains popped up. Stories like this connect the Cherokee of today with their rich and fascinating past.

The Cherokee people still hold a strong identity with their heritage. You can see how the red man lived over 225 years ago as Indian guides in native costumes lead you to primitive cabins and rustic arbours. You can watch Indian braves making a dug out canoe with fire and axe. Cherokee women mould ropes of clay into pots, weave baskets, and demonstrate the ancient art of finger weaving.

Inside the large exhibition centre, the Cherokee history, culture, social background and rituals, handed down from generation to generation, are on display.

Elsewhere you can see demonstrations of the timeworn methods of chipping flint into arrowheads, carving wooden spoons, combs and bowls, and pounding Indian corn into meal.

Among the many tribes inhabiting North America, the Cherokee had the first written language and by the early 1840's a Cherokee newspaper *"The Phoenix,"* was being circulated throughout the territory.

Another fact that surprises many visitors is that the Cherokee lived in log cabins, not tepees which were common among the nomadic tribes of the western plains.

THE MARCH OF PROGRESS

The North American Indians, of all tribes, were treated despicably by the white man. That's a fact of history. The white man's march of progress across the now United States left in its wake a trail of broken treaties, bloody massacres and tears.

Not all, if any, Indian tribes were naturally bloodthirsty savages. As I've mentioned in the first chapter of this book, the Cherokee certainly were not a savage people. They were a nation in their own right, highly civilised, farmers, and with their own national government. Yet, they too, were eventually driven west to no man's land in an inglorious episode that has now been well documented in *"The Trail of Tears."*

When Hernando deSoto first encountered the Cherokee, in 1540, he found a unified, peaceful nation of about 25,000 people. Some three hundred years later, almost to the year, the Cherokee became a divided nation with little remaining of their vast territory and national pride.

The Cherokee co-existed peacefully with early settlers, but the white man's lust for gold and land was all consuming and between 1684 and 1835, over thirty treaties chipped away at their original 135,000 square miles of Indian territory

The Cherokee issue was hotly debated in Congress for many years. Sadly, speeches on behalf of the Cherokee by such men as Henry Clay, Davy Crockett, Daniel Webster and other prominent statesmen fell on deaf ears. President Andrew Jackson, whose life was ironically saved by Cherokee Chief Junaluska, at the Battle of Horseshoe in 1812, was the one who signed the final "Removal Treaty."

THE TRAIL OF TEARS

Beginning in the spring of 1837 and continuing through the autumn of 1838, the Cherokee people were rounded up and corralled into hastily constructed stockades. So began the *"Trail of tears,"* a 1,200 mile journey to unfamiliar land.

Under the command of General Winfield Scott, over 600 wagons, steamers and keel boats moved about 16,000 Cherokee by land and by river. The infamous journey took between 105 and 189 days, and before they arrived in Oklahoma, torrential rains, ice storms, disease and broken heartedness had claimed the lives of at least 4,000 men, women and children.

A Georgia soldier who took part in the removal said *"I fought through the war between the States and have seen many men shot, but the Cherokee Removal was the cruellest work I ever knew."*

Will Thomas, an adopted Cherokee, purchased 56,000 acres which eventually became the Qualla Boundary where the Eastern Band of Cherokee Indians now live. The Eastern band of Cherokee are descendants of those who hid in the Great Smoky Mountains to avoid removal. Those who survived the journey to Oklahoma are the Western band.

In 1987 the United States Congress approved the recognition and development of the *"Trail of Tears National Historic Trail."* Several interpretive centres will be constructed along the routes in the near future.

A LOST PRIDE

Yet, as I walked around the Cherokee exhibition centre, I couldn't help thinking that any pride this once great nation of indigenous American people ever had, was now gone. The displays were some of the tackiest I have ever seen, and the videos, both in production values and technical quality were so bad that I couldn't watch them. Oh, there *was* history and culture there, but you had to be very interested and determined to dig for it.

One thing above all about the Indians struck me forcibly. It was the sadness on their faces and the lack of hope in their eyes. I don't think I've ever seen an Indian smile - perhaps they don't have much to smile about. Looking about their exhibitions and displays would seem to support that view.

Leaving Cherokee, we drove on again, over winding roads that defiant engineers had carved out of the sides of the mountains, through their forests and over their peaks.

PIGEON FORGE

At last we arrived in Pigeon Forge, an immediate disappointment! How anyone could have scarred so beautiful a landscape with so tatty a town I'll never know. This was the heart of the Great Smoky mountains, and yet it could have been Idaho, Missouri, Texas, Florida, anywhere.

Pigeon Forge, Tennessee, is one long street, lined on either side with gaudily painted shops and restaurants. Every third one seems to be *"The Home of Country Music,"* but I had never heard of any of the *"big stars"* they boasted. Dolly Parton has a theme park in Pigeon Forge. She's from the area, so I went to see it but when I heard the price, twenty five dollars, I decided against. I went instead to the Ernest Tubb music store and spent the money on something more lasting. And then I went to Shoney's, where *"BJ,"* our waitress, described the menu

"We've just recently put in a horseshoe bar and aw .. you've got soup and salad. There's about four different kinds of soup. Aw .. you've got salad on both sides of the bar and the lines when folk come in they go relatively fast. You can have anything that you want. You can get cottage cheese, tomatoes, pickles, aw .. you name it they got it on that bar there."

Shoneys, for those who've never been there, is one the best quick eating places in America. It's a franchised operation with branches all over the east and southern states. The food is always fresh, delicious, plentiful and cheap. In the mornings, they offer a one price, eat all you can, breakfast. A few years ago I took my eldest son, Jonathan, on a working visit to Alabama. We breakfasted at Shoneys every morning, determined to sample everything they had on offer, but we never managed to beat them. However, I do know a few people, with much larger appetites, who made sure that Shoneys didn't make a profit on the mornings they were there.

"BJ."

BJ came to our table immediately with glasses of water and a large pot of coffee. They drink lots of water and lots of coffee in America.

BJ was what the Americans would call *"a sweet little thing,"* small, slender, almost to the point of being thin. On her face, she had enough paint to paint a battleship and enough powder to blow it up. It wasn't very well applied either. She was sweet and polite, laughed at our jokes, was patient as we tried to pick our way through the strangely named dishes on the menu, but her expression revealed a hidden sadness.

It turned out that she had married at seventeen, was divorced a short time later and now was engaged again. However the thing about her that really caught my attention was her accent. It was the drawliest southern drawl I'd ever heard and I just wanted to keep her talking.

At Shoneys you can go up to the salad bar and help yourself as often as you like. So how often do customers normally yield to this temptation I wondered.

"Normally three or four times. Of course we like to see folks eat now. It's sort of like what my grandma used to say whenever folks would come to her house. If aw .. they didn't eat well then she thought like her cooking wasn't good. But if folks kept coming back to the table she knew that the food was good. So it was kinda like a compliment .. uh huh!"

Well if B.J.'s grandma had been watching us in Shoney's that day, at Pigeon Forge, she'd have been proud of us. We sampled the salad bar, more than once. We tried the chicken, and the biscuits, (small hot scones) and the gravy, and the french fries, and, it seemed, everything else they had on offer. BJ came back to our table, again and again, to refill our coffee cups. And each time she did so, when we said thanks, she replied with an *"Uh huh!"*

For me, there wasn't a lot to do in Pigeon Forge. I'm not into fun fairs, amusement arcades or shopping malls. The only things left were those country music emporiums. We went to see one of them, its name has long since escaped me. Around the walls of the small foyer hung pictures of country stars I'd never heard. Every once in a while individuals in pastel coloured, sequened suits ambled in and out through a small door which, I assumed, led to the main auditorium and the show. Since I have an inbuilt aversion to tourist traps I kept my dollars in my pocket again and moved on.

I'll always remember Pigeon Forge, but for the wrong reasons. There are many places in the U.S.A. I want to go and see again, and the Smokies is one of them, but I think I'll give Pigeon Forge a miss. Well, on second thoughts, I may just brace myself for the sake of Shoney's, and BJ, and her *"Uh huh!"*

six

The Capital of the Smokies

It's just a ten minute drive from Pigeon Forge to Gatlinburg, the capital of the Smoky Mountains, and a completely different town. Here's a place with charm, character and a mayor who was delighted to receive me, unannounced.

"James, as Mayor of Gatlinburg, at this time I'd like to officially present you with this certificate and make you an honorary, official Gatlinburg Mountaineer."

I'd gone to the tourist building in the centre of the town to ask if there was any possibility of speaking to someone who knew a little bit about the history of the place. I didn't have an appointment and so, more or less expected to be told to come back another day. However, the mature lady at the desk was polite and helpful. She made a telephone call and then directed me to a small, unassuming building a few streets away. I was to ask for Chuck Bradley.

Chuck was a tall, lean, clean shaven man in his late thirties or early forties. He wasn't what you'd describe as handsome but when he smiled the whole room felt the glow. It turned out that Chuck Bradley *was* the mayor. As he handed me my genuine imitation parchment scroll he proceed to read the full inscription.

A GATLINBURG MOUNTAINEER

"Be hit knowed to airy flatlander, foreigner, whatever might see here certificate that this here cousin, James K. McClelland are herewith recognised as an honorary Gatlinburg mountaineer."

"By virtue of such recognition the same are entitled to make licker from sun up to sun down; sample licker whether sun's up or sun's down; hunt coons from dark till daylight; participate in all day singin' and dinner on the grounds, (provide own dinner of course,) go barefoot, 'cept to church, but can kick off slippers during preachin'; leave ploughing when fish is a bitin'; and they is always honour bound to eat heartily of the many good fruits of the earth, such as, cornbread, taters and greens, chitlins, hominy grits, ham and red eye gravy, and good ole mountain dew.

"Be hit further knowed that if'n here this here cousin ever gets himself in a mess of trouble all he has to do is holler and we uns 'ill come a runnin' cause we uns sure do like a good feud and are always willin' to help our kin."

"This here document is made legal cause it's signed and sealed by me, the mayor and by Mr Randy Fiveash, our executive director of our chamber of commerce."

Chuck Bradley delivered his entire address in a slow southern drawl. I suspected he had laid this on especially for me, but when he finished and reverted back to his natural accent, I wasn't so sure. It didn't sound very much different.

THE ELIZABETHANS

I thanked Chuck for the great honour bestowed upon me and promised to fulfil its terms to the best of my ability. And then we got to talking about that accent of his.

"When you hear the Hill Billy dialect that's one of the purest strains of Elizabethan English, and many of our forefathers in this area were English and Scots-Irish."
Chuck was able to back up this claim with examples of the some of the words imported to the New World hundreds of years ago and still used today.

"Well the 'here's,' and the 'thar's,' that you will hear are still used by many of the old timers. And you'll still hear a little bit of that twang like it's evolved from one generation to another. It may change a little bit but it's still there, it's part of our heritage and we're very proud of it."

EARLY SETTLERS

The Smoky Mountain region was settled by English and Scots-Irish who came from the old country to escape religious persecution and famine - and in search of a new and better life. According to Chuck Bradley they happened upon the area for reasons other than mere chance.

"The beauty of the mountains attracted them and many of them said that this place reminded them so much of home. We have an annual event here, the Gatlinburg Highland Games, so we have a very, very strong heritage in this area."

Despite those Scots-Irish connections Gatlinburg has a distinctive continental European appearance. There's a Swiss or Bavarian look to the houses and shop fronts, with quaintly fashioned fascia boards and shuttered windows.

The first record of a family living the area now known as Gatlinburg is in the late 1790's. Jane Huskey Ogle, a widow, came to the valley during this time with her six sons and two daughters. Many of today's native families can trace their ancestry back to the Ogles. At the turn of that century another family also came into the area, that of Richard Reagan, who was the father of the first white child born in the valley.

Over the next three decades other families began to migrate to the valley from North Carolina and Virginia. Names like Watson, Trentham and Bales became familiar and many businesses and landmarks in the town today bear their names. Of todays 3,400 inhabitants, many native born citizens can trace their ancestry to the original Scots, Irish and English people.

FROM WHITE OAK FLATS TO GATLINBURG

Most of the early settlers were farmers, making their living from the soil. Others were craftsmen, supplying the increasing needs of the families moving into the area.

The village continued to grow and in 1935 became known as White Oak Flats. In 1855 Radford Gatlin entered the valley and opened the town's second store. The first had been opened by Noah Ogle in 1850. There are several stories of how the town came to be named after Mr. Gatlin but the main reason seems to have been because of his influence and ability to have the post office located in his store.

During the Civil war, the mountain people of East Tennessee for the most part remained loyal to the Union. The only notable conflict to occur in Gatlinburg happened in 1835 when Rebel forces built and occupied a small fort over looking the town on the "Burg Hill." A small number of whites and Indians fought a skirmish which was noted in history only because it was the last battle east of the Mississippi in which Indians participated.

THE FOUR SEASONS

Even though Chuck Bradley has lived in the Smokies all his life he was just as enthusiastic about the beauty of the place as I was.

"It really is a very unusual place because you do see a very distinct change of the four seasons. Beginning with spring visitors can watch as Mother Nature unfolds the landscape in all the colour and glory you would expect in a national forest of this size."

"When the temperatures begin to rise in the summer, there's nothing more relaxing than a cool mountain breeze. Refreshing mountain streams run right through the heart of Gatlinburg, providing the perfect setting for quiet nature walks or picnics under a shady tree."
By now I'm wishing I could come to Gatlinburg and the Smokies for a whole year, just to see Chuck's travelogue come to life.

"Then, if you've never been to Gatlinburg in the autumn, you're in for a special treat. Many of the national travel magazines feature Gatlinburg and the Great Smoky Mountains as one of the nation's most picturesque places to be when fall's crisp days arrive. The mountains turn from summer's rich greens to spectacular reds, yellows and oranges. It's truly nature's living colour show."

"And that just leaves winter. Well of course, winter is breathtaking throughout Gatlinburg and the Smokies. In the shops, restaurants and hotels

you'll find cosy fireplaces and friendly faces. There's skiing on the mountains, indoor ice skating, and our famous Smoky Mountain Lights when the town is festooned with thousands of coloured lamps of every hue. And of course we can't forget about the snow. We get over fifty inches of snow here every year and it just turns the place into an absolutely magnificent winter wonderland. It's fabulous. I love it!"

"Visitors also come here for the arts and crafts of this area. That's another thing that has been passed down through the heritage of the people. There's woodwork, pottery and other hand made crafts here and they all come from many, many generations back, from our mother country."

Chuck Bradley had certainly done a lot to whet my appetite for a return visit to the Smokies, but he wasn't finished yet.

"Here in Gatlinburg itself we have a lot to offer visitors, the shops, the restaurants and plenty of entertainment but, of course, people really come here for the beauty of the mountains. But more than that there's the Great Smoky Mountains National Park, and if you miss that you've missed the very best asset we have to offer."

"The park is five hundred thousand acres of nature at its best. And when you drive through this park you'll notice that we don't have a timber line. The whole mountains are covered in trees from the bottom right to the peaks and everything is so green. In fact many people tell us that it reminds them of the Emerald Isle and Scotland. It's a similar type beauty that you will find."

"There are many beautiful areas to visit in the Smoky Mountains National Park. Cades Cove is a great favourite with many people. Then a lot of people like to hike to Mount LeConte and, of course, inside the park there are some old homestead sites that are exactly as they were fifty years ago. So it's a great place to come to."

THE GREAT SMOKY MOUNTAINS NATIONAL PARK

Beginning with the Cherokee, then the settlers, and then the national park, human history has maintained a presence in the Smoky mountains for centuries. A lot of the history of that presence has been preserved in *"The Great Smoky Mountains National Park."* It's really a fabulous place to visit.

The Smokies are part of the Blue Ridge mountain range, which in turn is part of the southern Appalachians. The National Park straddles the Tennessee - North Carolina border for 60 miles. The Cherokee people called this area *Shaconage,* or "The Place of Blue Smoke."

The bluish mist, which clings to the mountains and fills the valleys, gives the park its name and remains its most distinctive feature. Over eight million people come to behold its wonders every year, and yet, because it's such an immense place, it never seems crowded.

The park was established in 1934, to protect the last remnant of the southern Appalachian forest, which once covered over four million acres. The government, wisely, stepped in to save what was left before the whole place was eliminated by logging and forest fire.

INTERNATIONAL RECOGNITION

The park's abundance and variety of animal and plant life have earned it a United Nations designation as an International Biosphere Reserve. There are more than thirteen hundred different flowering plants and a hundred and twenty-five types of trees.

Birds and wildlife occupy the park in abundance too. Over two hundred species of birds, about fifty types of fish, and sixty different mammals all make their home in the park. And, it's the salamander capital of the world. No less than twenty seven varieties of this wonderful little, lizard like creature can be spotted in the park - if you're sharp eyed enough.

All this animal, plant and wildlife is watched over devotedly by the men and women of the National Park Service who preserve this unique resource for locals and tourists alike.

The list of wildlife includes wild turkey, red wolf, muskrat, red fox, the southern flying squirrel, white-tailed deer and, most popular of all, the dreaded black bear.

THE BLACK BEAR

About 500 bears live in the park and they are powerful and intelligent creatures. They feed mainly on berries, nuts, seeds, acorns and insects, but they often seek human food. Bears have a keen sense of smell and are good at recognising shapes and colours. They can't read the labels but they do know that food often comes in cans, so it's not the first car door that's been prised open by a bear who thought that a can of tennis balls was a feast of tasty potato chips.

I dreaded the possibility of coming face to face with one of these hungry creatures, but Chuck Bradley was at pains to allay all my fears.

"If you respect wildlife it will respect you. Of course, if you run up on a bear and it's a mother and her cubs, never get close to the young cubs because it's going to be an instinct to the mother to try and protect her young. Many people think that they might be able to feed that young bear, just like they feed a dog. Well you have to remember that that is wildlife! It's not a tame animal. So as long as you respect them you'll never have any problems."

Thankfully, I didn't have the dubious pleasure of coming face to face with one of Chuck Bradley's black bears, although I did see lots of other examples of wild life. My abiding memory of the Great Smokies will be its majestic scenery, its friendly people and its music. We'll take a closer look at that Appalachian speciality, in the next chapter.

seven

The Music of Appalachia

Anthony Lampross, the ranger at Blackrock Overlook, in the hills above Clayton, Georgia looks off into the distance and muses about the music of the region.

"So much of it I believe is music that people can really relate to. Some of this hard rock and heavy metal, aw, if you can't even understand the words how can you understand the meaning of the songs. Aw, bluegrass and country music, on the other hand, is music that, in my opinion, is straight from the heart. It deals with the problems and the joys of just ordinary, everyday folk, and ordinary, everyday people that listen to it can appreciate that, and it means something to them."

PSALMS & PICKIN'

It's often puzzled me why someone like myself, raised in a Psalm singing, Presbyterian tradition, should have such a liking for, an affinity even, with country music. The Appalachian mountains of Virginia, North Carolina, Georgia and Tennessee were settled hundreds of years ago by people of my ancestry; those same Psalm singers from Scotland and Northern Ireland.

I doubt if there were many fiddle players among them, and I'm pretty certain they weren't the kind of people to go to a Saturday night hoe down, or barn dance. So why then has the area which they settled, the Appalachians, become the birth place and the nursery for the music which has now taken the world by storm?

I'm not sure I can provide the answer to that question. Indeed, I'm not sure that anyone can. But what I can say with a degree of certainly is that, there's something about those Appalachian mountains which inspires music that people, everywhere, want to listen to.

"Sittin' on the front porch
On a Sunday afternoon,
In a straight backed chair on two legs,
Leaned against the wall.
Watch the kids a playing
with June bugs on a string
And chase the glowing firefly
When evenin' shadows fall."

"In my Tennessee mountain home
Life is a sweet as a baby's sigh.
In my Tennessee mountain home
The crickets sing in the fields nearby."
("In my Tennessee Mountain Home." Dolly Parton.)

DOLLY PARTON

Dolly Parton, who wrote and sings *"In my Tennessee Mountain Home,"* is a Tennessee mountain girl herself, but as soon as she got the chance, she said good-bye to the mountains and headed for the bright lights of Nashville, to fame and fortune. Chuck Bradley, a mountain man himself, gave me the details.

"Dolly Parton was born in an area not for from here. Gatlinburg is approximately thirteen miles from Severaville. Dolly has also opened a theme park at Pigeon Forge, it's called 'Dollywood,' and of course her entire family is still in the area."

Gatlinburg is the capital of the Great Smoky Mountain region of east Tennessee, and Chuck Bradley, its mayor, is very proud of the musical traditions.

"One of our most recent additions to Gatlinburg, Helen Cornelius, who has recorded with Jim Ed Brown, has a local club called 'Nashville Sound,' and

she and her husband, Gerry Garing were so taken with the area, and its beauty, that they fell in love with it. Helen frequently tells the story that, she was tired of touring all over the country and wanted to come off the road. So, when she and her husband saw this place, as I say, they fell in love with it. Now they run this club here in Gatlinburg where Helen, herself, entertains at least one night every week.

A PROUD HERITAGE

"You'll see a lot of Bluegrass music in this area. We have one local group in which one of my fellow commissioners, Fred McMan, sings. They're called "The Mountain Travellers," and they have helped to preserve the heritage of bluegrass music in the area.

"In the 1950's and 1960's the thing that made this area attractive to people was the number of different musical groups it boasted. You still see some in Gatlinburg. There are more in Pigeon Forge as it has grown up, and really the whole county is very, very proud of that type of heritage."

KATE STURGILL

Over in Rabun Gap, Georgia, in the Blue Ridge Mountains of north east Georgia, George Reynolds teaches music at the local county high school.

"Well I did research several years ago about a woman who was a song writer up in Virginia. Everybody around there said 'Now if you wanted to talk to a real folk singer, talk to Kate Sturgill.'

Kate Sturgill did songs that she picked up out of tabloids and magazines and stuff. There were sentimental songs and gospel songs, some with known authors. You know I thought folk-songs had to be something that was passed down through the generations and that the authors were long forgotten. I wanted to find out why people felt that what she was doing was folk music."

THE THREE BASIC THEMES

George moves to the blackboard and picks up the chalk.

I suppose, being a teacher, he can better illustrate the point he makes with a diagram.

"What I found was that she wrote songs on three basic themes; the old home place - neighbours and loved ones - and heaven."

For his masters degree, George made a thorough study of the music of the Appalachians, and especially of Bluegrass. In the classroom he explains to his students the connection between home, neighbours and church, a theme that runs all the way through the music of the mountains.

"People frequently learn how to play music at home, amongst their neighbours, and in church. Those also tend to be the places where people play. Those three institutions are primarily what sticks it all together. And if you listen to bluegrass music one of the things that sets it apart is, you know, songs like - George breaks into song - *"Mother's not dead, she only a sleepin.' Mother's gone on to heaven and one of these days I'll meet her in heaven too. That age old theme runs through and through bluegrass music."*

THE WHITE MAN'S SPIRITUAL

I wondered if perhaps bluegrass music is the white equivalent of the Negro spiritual. George's broad smile told me that he liked the idea.

"I think that's a grand idea! In terms of function it helps validate important community structures. It helps remind people of what's important in the community. I think it helps people relieve a lot of their anxieties. People like to cry as well as to laugh, and a lot of the songs I've been listening to since I was a kid, and a lot of the songs that I do, fit into that category.

"You know people from outside of this community say to me 'Man, those songs are so morose! They're all about somebody dying or something.' Well, you know, that maybe so." - he chuckles - *"They maybe, but it's good to work out sorrows. It's good to work out a lot of bad days by singing songs that express those feelings. Songs like,*

"Tempted and tried we're oft' made to wonder
Why it should be, thus, all the day long.
While there are others , living around us,
Never molested, though in the wrong."

"Well, of course, the chorus gives, if not an answer to that conundrum, at least something to hope for in a better future."

"Farther along we'll know all about it,
Farther along we'll understand why.
Cheer up my brother, live in the sunshine,
We'll understand it all, bye and bye."

"Most of these songs about death are also about hope as well, and I think,
from what I know about African American spirituals, they were songs which
dealt with sorrow and they were incredibly intense, incredibly emotional, and
although they were about sorrow they also became uplifting, especially the way
African American spirituals came to be used in the civil rights movement. They
became functional, not only as songs that could lift people up, but songs that
could bind people together. Yes I think the connection between bluegrass songs
and African American spirituals is a perfectly logical one. I wish I'd thought
of that myself"

IMMIGRATION

Between 1800 and 1840 some one and a half million people, mostly from
Europe, settled in America. In the next two decades immigration accelerated
and a further five and a half million people came to the new world. Again they
were mainly from Europe, from all parts of it. As well as the Scots and the Irish,
there were English, Germans, Italians, Dutch, Greeks, Swedes, Russians, even
Turks. And then from the far east there were the Chinese, the Japanese and the
other Orientals.

All these peoples came to America in search of a better life, and by dint of
circumstances they were thrown together in places of work; the mines, the
railroads and the lumber camps.

But though they had left their homelands far behind, they brought with them
their cultures, the food, the dress - and the music.

THE MELTING POINT

"The melting pot is a metaphor that's been used quite a bit. In fact, I've also
heard people use 'salad bowl,' as well. Obviously there would have been a
mixing of community cultures, and sometimes the dominant culture completely
squelched some immigrants sense of their background.

"My mum used to teach school in the coalfields, back in the depression. She had a considerable number of kids whose mother didn't speak any English, but whose father would speak nothing but English, and who forbade the kids to speak in Italian, or Hungarian, or Greek, or whatever. His fear was that if they kept speaking their mother's tongue they wouldn't be able to make it in this English speaking world.

"There's probably a considerable amount of suppression of European family culture that went on, like that. But there's also the distinct possibility that many of the things brought in by the immigrants were, in fact, contributing factors to what eventually became bluegrass and country music.

There's a considerable amount of African American musical influence. You've the banjo and you've got the whole idea that they call it 'bluegrass.' There's definitely an influence of African music in what we call bluegrass. That's what makes it sound different from what we call old time music."

MUSIC FROM AFRICA

This idea of African influence was completely new to me. I'd expected the influences to be all Scots-Irish or English but George Reynolds was pretty sure of himself and his facts.

"Well, Africa, via the Caribbean and the deep south, and African Americans who were banjo players that worked on the railroads and worked in the coal mines. There were a considerable number of African Americans who were working along side of, or in the same communities with the European folks and there was a sharing of things. I've run in to white folks that were singing Robert Johnson style blues, up in the coalfields. There was a lot of mixing of cultures in the coalfields. A lot of immigrants came in to work in the coal mines and there were a considerable amount of different nationalities and cultures up there"

The mixing of cultures brought the intermingling of musical styles, and with that, the sharing of instruments. From Scotland and Ireland came the fiddle; from Germany the accordion; from Sweden the dulcimer; and from the African Americans the banjo. When people came together the musical instruments came together too, to make a new music forged in the furnace of life's experiences.

"A miner was leaving his home for his work,
When he heard his little child scream.
Then he ran to the side of the little girl's bed,
She said, 'Daddy, I've had such a dream!'

"Oh, Daddy don't go to the mines today,
For dreams have so often come true.
Oh, Daddy, my Daddy please don't go away,
For I never could live without you."
("The Dream of the Miner's Child." Doc Watson.)

THE FORGING OF CULTURES

That song *"The Dream of the Miner's child"* performed by Doc Watson, is just one example of the kind of new music that came out of men being brought together, in thousands, to work in the coal mines and on the railroads. George Reynolds explained.

"The industrial revolution in America, although it may have started in the north, came to Appalachia and settled in. And a lot of the wealth in the northern industrial centres was actually channelled out of Appalachia on the railroads; all the timber and coal and minerals.

The heavy industries came in the 1870's and '80's and '90's, and a lot of times, little communities that might have had, maybe five hundred people in a county, would have had ten or fifteen thousand people within ten years time. Now that was an enormous turnover. There was lots of heavy industry, lots of danger, lots of chaos, lots of people getting hurt. The legal system really wasn't set up for ten thousand people, there was maybe only one sheriff in the whole county, with people settling disputes on their own by just taking the law into their own hands.

"It was pretty chaotic from everything I've been able to tell from the old timers that grew up during that time, and yes there were conditions that set up sentimental music and gospel music to be important parts of the community culture."

In the song *"The Springhill Disaster,"* Bill Clifton and the Dixie Mountain Boys relate the story of an actual pit tragedy, one of the constant terrors for families involved in the coal mines.

"The twenty third of October, we'll remember that day,
Down the shaft underground in our usual way,
In the Cumberland pit how the rafters crashed down,
And the black hell closed round us way down in the ground.

"Now when the news reached our good neighbours nearby,
The rescue work started, their hopes were still high.
But the last bit of hope, like our lamps, soon burned dim.
In that three foot high dungeon we joined in a hymn.
"In that dark, black hole in the ground ....
("The Springhill Disaster." Bill Clifton & The Dixie Mountain Boys.)

RELIGIOUS UNDERTONES

It's interesting to note that, while *"The Springhill Disaster,"* isn't a gospel song, it has very definite religious undertones. When tragedy strikes even the toughest living, hardest drinking, meanest men will join in the hymn singing. They too, have to meet their maker someday.

According to George Reynolds, when bluegrass music came along a little later, it could have been designed for those mountain people.

"In the forties, when bluegrass was originated with the Monroe brothers, it just fitted right into community culture which was waiting for it. In fact, there were lots of old time tunes about before the Monroe brothers came on the scene. You know, songs about sweetheart and home, that sort of thing. The Carter family, Jimmy Rogers, the Blue Sky Boys and all those folks that were predecessors of bluegrass had been singing these songs for years. That sentimentality and that religious piety, that is ingrained in old tyme bluegrass, fits right in, and I think, from the point of view of a folklorist, it had its functionality in helping people bring order to a chaotic life"

If we're to believe the rags to riches stories of many of the big names of country music, living in those mountains was a life of poverty and despair. No wonder they couldn't wait to get out of the place. Yet it's a strange paradox that the very   place they can't wait to get away from is the one they're so fond of dreaming about in the loneliness of a big city, so fond of   romanticising in their songs.

STARS IN THEIR EYES!

According to Chuck Bradley, the Appalachian mountains are still full of little, would be, Dolly Partons, anxious to escape the hills, to get to Nashville, and to make it big in country music. And he maintains, it's the mountains that provide the inspiration.

"At the Gatlinburg Inn, which is one of the oldest establishments in town, the song 'Rocky Top,' was written in room 388. It was co-written by Boudleaux and Felice Bryant. Felice Bryant is now a resident of Gatlinburg, her husband passed away about three or four years ago.

"But that summer, while they were here, they wrote the songs 'Rockytop,' 'Love Hurts,' that the group 'Nazareth,' recorded and also 'Come Live with Me,' that Roy Clarke recorded.

"So when you start looking back over the past several years you'll see that the mountains have provided the inspiration that a lot of people needed to get the creative juices flowing. So I truly think that if you want to know what the biggest asset to this area is, it's the beauty of the mountains"

And perhaps that inspiration provided by the mountains is best summed up in one of my favourite Appalachian songs, sung by two of the great Bill Monroe's former Smoky Mountain Boys, Lester Flatt and Mac Wiseman, *"The Bluebirds singing for me."*

"Tonight I'm far from the Blue Ridge mountains,
Far from my home back in the hills.
But I'm going back to the Blue Ridge mountains
These memories, they haunt me still.

"There's a bluebird singin' in the Blue Ridge mountains
Calling me back to my home.
Oh I can hear the bluebirds callin',
Callin' me back to my home."

I never did get to hear the bluebirds singing in the Blue Ridge Mountains, or in any other part of the Appalachians for that matter. But I didn't need to. Their beauty and mystery call to me every day.

eight

From the Appalachians to the World

*"W*hen you start looking back over the past several years you'll see that the mountains have provided the inspiration that a lot of people needed to get the creative juices flowing. So I truly think that if you want to know what the biggest asset to this area is, it's the beauty of the mountains"*

Mayor Chuck Bradley, of Gatlinburg, Tennessee, extolling the virtues of the Great Smoky Mountains and their capacity to inspire music which all the world, well, almost all the world, loves to sing.

It was to those same Smoky mountains, in the summer of 1927, that a young record producer sallied forth on what was to become an historic mission.

Commercial country music was barely four years old. It was a bawling infant though, and the record sales of people like *Fiddlin' John Carson, Uncle Dave Macon and Riley Puckett,* had convinced the big New York record companies that there was another kind of gold in *"Them thar hills."*

RALPH PEER

Ralph Peer, of the Victor Talking Machine Company, made the long journey from New York to Bristol, on the Tennessee - Virginia border, and set up a temporary recording studio. Adverts had been placed in the local papers and musicians came from miles around to show off their talents to the young executive from New York.

It must have been an exciting and interesting time in the history of American music. I'd surely like to have been there.

Ralph Peer, a 35 year old native of Kansas City, was a pioneer in the new technique of *"on-location,"* recording. He had grown up with the record industry, and in 1923 had travelled to Atlanta, Georgia to record the famous efforts of Fiddlin' John Carson.

He arrived in Bristol, Tennessee on the 21st July 1927. Along with him were his wife, Anita and two engineers named Eckhart and Lynch. They brought a car load of brand new recording equipment, the latest technology available, produced by Western Electric and provided by Peer's employers.

A former furniture store at 408 State Street (the street which divided Tennessee from Virginia) was leased, and they began to prepare the second and third stories for recording. The walls were hung with blankets, to deaden unwanted reflections, and a tower was built to house the pulleys and weights that would drive the recording turntable. A platform was erected for the singers, too.

SEARCHING FOR HILLBILLYS

Ralph Peer had already scouted the area earlier that year and had the first week's list of artists lined up. The deal was that he would record them on the spot, pay them $50 a selection and a royalty of about two and a half cents per side. He was looking for hillbilly music, blues and gospel.

However, he needed artists for the second week of recording. An advertisement in the Sunday paper hadn't generated much response, so Peer invited a reporter for the local paper to watch Ernest Stoneman and Eck Dunford record *"Skip to Ma Lou."* A front page story appeared in that evening's local *"Bristol News Bulletin,"* and the most interesting part of that report was the astounding fact that Stoneman got $100 a day for his labours, and his sideman, Dunford, $25 a day.

The report worked like dynamite. The next day Peer was deluged with long distance phone calls from all over the surrounding mountain area. Groups of singers who had never visited Bristol in the entire lifetime, arrived by bus, train, horse and buggy, even on foot.

In a matter of hours Peer had gone from a famine to a feast, and soon he had to lay on special night time recording sessions to accommodate the new talent.

THE BRISTOL SESSIONS

The seventy-six recordings produced at the Bristol sessions form an almost perfect cross section of early country music - from fiddle tunes to blues, from deep-rooted ballads to gospel songs.

Among the finds uncovered on this unique occasion were the great Jimmy Rodgers and the Carter Family, people who were to become big stars in later years, and whose music has influenced country, bluegrass, and folk ever since.

The recordings of Jimmie Rodgers and The Carter Family highlighted two of country music's most imitated styles, two of its most appealing impulses.

Rodgers represented the tradition of the rambling man, so attractive to country music's folk ancestors and fascinating to much of its audience.

The ex-railroad man gave the impression that he had been everywhere and had experienced life to the full. In his history of country music *"Country Music U.S.A.,"* Bill C. Malone says *"Rodgers' music conveyed a similar openness of spirit, a willingness to experiment, and a receptivity to alternative styles."*

THE CARTER FAMILY

The Carter Family, on the other hand, stood for the home and the family, stability, a theme just as attractive as that of the rambler.

When the Carters sang they evoked images of the old country church, of Mama and Papa, the family fireside, and the green fields of home, often far away.

About half of the Carter family's repertoire was gospel and they're still claimed as a gospel group, even today. They were to became the most important of country music's dynasties.

Alvin Pleasant Carter (A.P.) was born at Maces Spring, Scott County, Virginia, in 1891. He was brought up in a strict Christian environment and learned to love the old fashioned religious songs sung in church. It was there too that he first heard the four part harmonies that have become so much a part of country gospel.

He also came to like the sound of the fiddle which his parents rejected as an instrument of the devil. He had to wait quite a while before he could afford to buy one.

Sara Carter, whom A.P. married in 1915, came from Copper Creek, also in Scott County. She was an accoimplished instrumentalist and a good singer. After their marriage their home in Maces Spring became something of a local attraction because Sara and A.P. were already singing together.

MOTHER MAYBELLE

The third member of the Carter family was Maybelle, also from Virginia. She married A.P.'s brother Ezra in 1926. Although some ten or eleven years younger than Sara when the Bristol sessions were held, she was already a talented autoharp and banjo player. It was, however, her guitar playing that made her name great.

Indeed Maybelle Carter, *"Mother Maybelle,"* as she's affectionately referred to, gave her name to a guitar style, her own "thumb brush," technique, in which she played rhythm with the fingers and picked out the melody at the same time with the thumb. The classic example of this unique style, and one that every fledgeling guitarist seeks to copy, is her rendering of *"Wildwood Flower."* There is just nothing like it.

Sara and Maybelle did the singing on most of the Carter Family's recordings, with A.P. joining in with the bass or baritone line, when he felt like it.

"Down away by the waters so blue
 They carried the beautiful child
To its own tender mother, its sister and brother,
 Little Moses looked happy and smiled
"His mother so good, did all that she could
 To rear him and teach him with care.
His mother so good, done all that she could
 To rear him and teach him with care."

A FADING DREAM!

Bill C. Malone in his history of country music says that the Carter family sang of an America that was gradually disappearing. That America had been fading since before the Carters were children, though its vision may have burned brighter in the rural south than anywhere else in the nation. Songs about wandering boys, abandoned mothers, dying orphans and forsaken lovers had a special appeal for people who saw the stable world of their parents disintegrating around them.

That emphasis on home and mother and old fashioned morality lived in country music long after the Carter family dissolved their commercial partnership. And it's one that the industry has continued to cultivate.

JIMMIE ROGERS

It's interesting to note that when Ralph Peer first listened to, and recorded, Jimmie Rogers he felt the material he was singing wasn't old enough. Rogers was doing fairly new pop songs and Peer asked him for something older. Rogers came up with his version of an old first World War song, *"The Soldier's Sweetheart."* To show off Rodger's yodelling talents he did *"Sleep, Baby Sleep,"* an old vaudeville song from the 1860s and one which had already been recorded by several other singers.

"Sleep, baby sleeping, close you're bright eyes,
   Listen to your mother, dear, sing these lullabies."
(*"Sleep, baby sleep."* Jimmie Rodgers)

The Bristol sessions, as they've become known, were proof, if proof was needed, that the music of the Appalachian mountains, so much a part of life to the locals who lived there, could also appeal to a wider audience and be commercially successful.

A MUSICAL REVOLUTION

The music of Jimmie Rodgers and the Carter Family took off. Many other new musicians were discovered, or went knocking on the doors of the big recording companies, looking for that elusive *"break."* For some it came. For many it didn't - and they went back into those same hills, disillusioned and disappointed.

The music was changing too, developing, progressing, being refined, made more commercially attractive, and being given new names, like *"bluegrass."*

"I traced her little footprints in the snow,
I found her little footprints in the snow.
I bless that happy day that Nellie lost her way
For I found her when the snow was on the ground."
(*"Footprints in the Snow."* Bill Monroe)

THE BIRTH OF BLUEGRASS!

To the uninitiated, bluegrass music is as old as the hills, a time honouring, surviving piece of folk Americana. Traditional, authentic, unamplified, hill country music, referred to by most people as bluegrass, is still in demand today and its almost entirely due to the pioneering efforts of one man, Bill Monroe, known everywhere, quite rightly, as "The Father of Bluegrass."

"Well he was clearly the leader of the band who first called the music bluegrass and who gave bluegrass the official formula that we use to play it. By that I mean the instrumentation, the way people take different breaks, the speed, the harmonies"

George Reynolds is a bluegrass student, a member of a bluegrass band "The Foxfire Boys," and a music teacher at Rabun County High School, in north east Georgia.

"I'm sure that any style of music that developed and called something new, like "Rock and Roll," or "Jazz," is bound to have a history that's very important. But there are fundamentally important people who happen to be at the right place, at the right time when it occurs. I think Mr. Monroe gave the music a particular personal flavour which it has maintained over the years. Although there are other musicians who have added their personal flavour to it too. There's all kinds of different types of bluegrass as well"

"A pathway of teardrops to show you the way
If you ever wanna come back to me.
You know dear that I'll cry both night and day
Since you told me you'd never be free."
("A Pathway of Teardrops." Wayne Walker & Webb Pierce)

Other types of bluegrass there may have been, in fact there were, but it was Bill Monroe who, with his *"Bluegrass Boys,* gave it its unique, much imitated style and, of course, its name.

THE FATHER OF BLUEGRASS!

William Smith Monroe was born in Rosine, Kentucky, in 1911. His mother Melissa and uncle Pendelton Vandiver were accomplished musicians, fiddle players, and the whole family was devoted to church music and shape note singing.

Bill was attracted to many musical forms, including blues and spirituals, as well as the old time mountain music of the region. Uncle Pen taught young Bill to play the guitar, mandolin and fiddle, and soon the boy was accompanying his uncle to dances, with older brothers Charlie, who played the guitar, and Birch, the fiddle. As a result of the brothers' choice of instruments Bill finally settled on the mandolin.

The three Monroe brothers formed a string band ensemble and in that epochal year of 1927 performed their first radio broadcasts. In 1930 they had a successful recording of *"Kentucky Waltz,"* and that was followed later with *"Blue Grass Ramble."*

In 1936 Charlie and Bill formed a double act and toured several states including Iowa, Nebraska, North Carolina and South Carolina. The brothers, however, didn't get on well together and, after several serious disputes, each went his separate way.

THE BLUEGRASS BOYS

Bill formed a new band in 1938 and, since his native state is renowned for its unique blue grass region, he named the group in its honour. *"The Blue Grass Boys,"* were to become the most famous exponents of the new musical genre and, at the same time, give it its name.

To a lot of people *"The Blue Grass Boys,"* were just another string band. However, they were a string band with a difference - Bill Monroe. Monroe was the driving cog, and all the other musicians revolved around him. With his mandolin setting the beat and rhythm for the band, he did most of the singing too, usually taking the solo part on the verse and then sweeping up to that unforgettable high tenor harmony for the choruses.

Monroe's tenor singing, often referred to as the "high, lonesome sound," set a standard for which bluegrass musicians still strive. One of the best compliments any bluegrass singer can be given is for people to say "Why he can sing as high as Bill Monroe!"

EARL SCRUGGS

In 1945 a new, young musician joined *"The Blue Grass Boys."* Earl Scruggs brought a sensational technique to the five string banjo. It made his own name pre-eminent among country and folk musicians and established bluegrass music as a national phenomenon.

However, as far as George Reynolds is concerned, Bill Monroe is the man who deserves the credit for the music that has had feet tapping and fingers drumming for decades.

"He put a stamp on it. But you'd have to say that Earl Scruggs' Banjo style added an enormously important identity to it. Had it not been for Earl Scruggs the music might not be what we think of as Bluegrass today. Every once in a while in history there's a certain kind of magic that happens and, all of a sudden, bang, there's born this wonderful form of music that seems to be unique, although you can identify its predecessors."

"You know, it's like when a star is born in the universe. The gasses and stuff are all out there and then one day it just starts to heat up and burn. We owe a good measure of respect to Bill Monroe, and a good measure of respect to other people as well. But I think he put his stamp on it, and I would be willing to give him credit where credit's due"

WESTERN SWING

Another big star of the nineteen thirties and forties was Bob Wills, the man who put the *"Western,"* into country and western. Leading his *"Light Crust Dough Boys,"* later to become *"The Texas Playboys,"* Wills fronted an outfit that had little competition as the most popular western band of all time.

"Deep within my heart lies a melody,
A song of old San Antone.
Where in dreams I live with a memory
Beneath the stars all alone.

It was there I found beside the Alamo
Enchantment strange as the blue up above
A moonlit path that only she would know
It hears my broken song of love."
("Rose of San Antone." Bob Wills)

Bob Wills and his Texas Playboys played a brand of music they called "*Western Swing*," and soon people all across the southern states were dancing to it. However, there was still bluegrass, and country, and the more simple music of the mountains. Carroll Lee, himself at first a musician, and then a pioneer radio broadcaster, grew up in those days, and with that music.

PICKIN' AND A GRINNIN'

"Back in the thirties we had a lot of mountain type music, or Irish oriented music; jigs and things of that nature. Then we had what they termed "Western," music, country and western. This came from Bob Wills and his Texas Playboys; that was a very prominent outfit. Another one that I liked was "The Sons of the Pioneers." That was a group that featured Roy Rogers. I find it hard to describe them, they were so melodious, and harmonious. They just made chills run over you. I suppose one of their best known numbers would have to be "Blue Shadows on the Trail." I liked that song."

"Shades of night are fallin',
As the wind begins to sigh
And the world is silhouetted
'Gainst the sky.

"Blue shadows on the trail,
Blue moon shining through the trees
And the plaintiff wail from the distance
Comes a driftin' on the evening breeze."

"Move along blue shadows, move along.
Soon the dawn will come and you'll be on your way,
Until the darkness sheds its vail,
There'll be blue shadows on the trail.
("Blue Shadows on the Trail." Sons of the Pioneers)

BEATING STRAWS

Carroll Lee has some childhood memories of one of the earliest forms of accompaniment in mountain music, beating straws.

"Now my grandfather, he played the fiddle back then and I remember when I was just a kid he played the fiddle and let me beat straws. You took broom straws and beat the strings as the fiddler played, as he pulled the bow back and forward over the strings They called that the beaten strings. You were beating the violin strings because he was holding the chords, and I, as a small child, had the rhythm to beat the strings on his fiddle.

"Back then you had dances in the homes about the community. There were other places where the people met on a Saturday night and you'd have a fiddle and a banjo. That would be the instrumentation and they would sing and dance there till midnight."

"As I say my grandfather played the fiddle, and then at a later time I also played the fiddle, hoe-down fiddle we called it. We played Irish tunes, jigs, reels and it was very evident that the music had an Irish influence"

THE IRISH INFLUENCE

With all his personal knowledge and experience of the mountain music scene from all those years ago, I wondered if Carroll Lee had any idea how the fiddle playing developed from the folk *"Diddle de de,"* style to the bluegrass and country styles which I can only describe as more of a sawing, singing fiddle.

"I don't know just who developed that down through the years but we had quite a number of fellows that came from all parts of the country into Nashville, the country capital of the world, I reckon. They had a programme going up there since the 1920s "The Grand Ole Opry," and some of the folks I played with wound up there. But there is an influence that comes from the Louisiana area, from around New Orleans. You got blues, and country, and bluegrass all interpolated into a strain and it is just remarkable. But the Appalachian area, naturally, is going to give you your Irish flavour."

That there's an Irish flavour to the music is certain, and that they're proud of the connection with the 'oul country is equally certain. Wherever I went people seemed anxious to convince me of their Scots-Irish roots. The people who left these shores for the new world were tough, hardy, pioneering spirits. They endured great hardship, and suffered many tragedies, carving out a new life from the rugged hills of Appalachia. All of that is poured out in their music and songs. Perhaps that's why they're so universally accepted. Carroll Lee expounds the idea.

"It depicts how people feel. People, regardless of where they're from have the same feelings, and it's just a matter of expressing those feelings to people everywhere. I mean, country music is the most expressive music there is. It tells a story. It tells how you feel and what you've got to do about it"

"As you read this letter that I write to you.
Sweetheart I hope you'll understand
That you're the only love I knew.
Please forgive me if you can.

"Sweetheart I beg you to come home tonight
I'm so blue and all alone
I promise that I'll treat you right.
Love, Oh love, Oh please come home."
("Love please come home."
Don Reno, Red Smiley & the Tennessee Cutups.)

The story of country music is a never ending one. It's been the subject of a great many books and, I suppose, it'll spawn a few more as time goes on. That the Appalachian mountains spawned the music, both bluegrass and country, there is little doubt.

nine

Gospel Country

"It's G.L.O.R.Y. to know I'm S.A.V.E.D.
I'm H.A.P.P.Y. because I'm F.R. double E.
I once was B.O.U.N.D. in the chains of S.I.N.
But it's V.I.C.T.O.R.Y. to know I've Christ within.

"Some folks jump up and down all night and D.A.N.C.E.
While others go to church to show their brand new H.A.T.
And on their face they put great gobs of P.A.I.N.T.
And then they'll have the brass to say they're S.A.V.E.D.

"Well I see some girls in this town who are so N.I.C.E.
They do their hair in the latest style that's B.O.B.E.D.
They go to parties every night drink W.I.N.E.
And then they'll have the nerve to say they're S.A.V.E.D.

"Well I know a man, I think his name's B.R.O.W.N.
He prays for prohibition and he votes for G.I.N.
He helps to put the poison in his neighbours C.U.P.
And then he'll have the brass to say he's S.A.V.E.D.

"Well it's G.L.O.R.Y. to know I'm S.A.V.E.D.
I'm H.A.P.P.Y. because I'm F.R. double E.
I once was B.O.U.N.D. in the chains of S.I.N.
But it's V.I.C.T.O.R.Y. to know I've Christ within."

CHURCH INFLUENCE!

Most country music historians and commentators agree that one of the biggest, if not the biggest, influences on country music was the church. It was in church, especially the churches of the southern Bible belt, that many of the singers learned the rudiments of their music. It was there that they first heard singing in four part harmony. It was there that they learned to read music, very often by the shaped note system. And it was there that the fundamentals of home and family, based on the simple teachings of the Bible, were drummed into them. It's little wonder then that country music has given rise to so many songs on Bible themes.

"I'm using my Bible for a road map.
The ten commandments tell me what to do.
The twelve disciples are my road signs,
And Jesus is there to pull me through.

"There'll be no detours in heaven.
No rough roads along the way.
I'm using my Bible for a road map,
My last stop is heaven some sweet day."

"I'm using my Bible for a road map.
The children of Israel used it too.
They crossed the red sea of destruction,
And God was there to pull them safely through.

"There'll be no detours in heaven.
No rough roads along the way.
I'm using my Bible for a road map,
My last stop is heaven some sweet day."
("I'm Using my Bible for a Roadmap.")

THAT LITTLE OLD COUNTRY CHURCH!

As I write I can think of at least four songs that hark back to that little country church where the singing was always full hearted, the preaching always clear and forthright, and the fellowship with those of like precious faith always warm and sympathetic.

Jim and Jessie McReynolds sing about *"A Little White Church."* Tennessee Ernie Ford, who always closed every T.V. show with a gospel number sang about *"The Church in the Wildwood,"* as have dozens of other artists. George Hamilton IV, himself a committed Christian, sings about *"The Old Country Church."* And just recently I came across a new one to me on the *"little church in the country,"* theme, Ricky Skaggs and the *"Little Mountain Church House."*

"There's a little mountain church
In my thoughts of yesterday.
Where friends and family gathered for the Lord.
There an old fashioned preacher
Taught the straight and narrow way
For what few coins the congregation could afford.

"Dressed in all our Sunday best
We sat on pews of solid oak,
And I remember how our voices filled the air.
How Mama sounded like an angel
On those high soprano notes
And when the roll is called up yonder I'll be there.

"Lookin' back now that little mountain church house
Has become my life's corner stone.
It was there in that little mountain church house
I first heard the word I based my life upon."

"At the all day Sunday singin's
And dinner on the ground.
Many were the souls that were revived.
While the brothers and the sisters
Who've gone on to glory land,
Slept in peace in the maple grove nearby.

"Lookin' back now that little mountain church house
Has become my life's corner stone.
It was there in that little mountain church house
I first heard the word I based my life upon."
("Little Mountain Church House." Ricky Skaggs.)

"Little Mountain Church House," must surely epitomise everything nostalgic about growing up in the southern Bible belt. As George Reynolds points out it includes all the elements that are near and dear to the hearts of mountain folk; the home, family and friends and the prospect of heaven.

NOSTALGIA AND MONEY

And that nostalgia for the church and religion of childhood, or the old homestead, stayed with country music when it went in search of commercial success, to Nashville, Tennessee.

Most people assume that music is the primary industry of Nashville. In fact it's not, and it never has been. The main industry of *"Music City,"* is religious printing and publishing. The Methodist, Presbyterian and Baptist Churches, to name but a few, all have their main publishing houses in Nashville.

Gospel tracts, music books, hymnals and Bibles roll off their presses, at a phenomenal rate, every year.

The music industry moved to Nashville in the forties and fifties and, at first, it wasn't well received by the churches. The southern states of America are well known as the *"Bible Belt,"* an area of ardent religious fervour, deep rooted fundamentalist doctrine and the bastion of the old time religion. The faithful saints in Nashville didn't take kindly to *"worldly music,"* making its home in their midst. Over the years, however, it seems they've become used to it.

LUKE THE DRIFTER!

Gospel music back in those days was part of the country music scene. There was country gospel, and bluegrass gospel, as well as standard, traditional gospel music that was sung in church on Sunday. You could go into a store or cafe where there was a juke box and listen to Bill Monroe or Hank Williams doing their regular Saturday night country songs. But you could also listen to Hank Williams as *"Luke the Drifter,"* doing one of his gospel numbers, such as *"I saw the Light,"* or *"House of Gold."*

One of the first ever country gospel recordings was made by Ernest "Pop" Stoneman. For Ulster people it's interesting to note that Stoneman's first recording, made on a wax cylinder, was a song about the Titanic. His first gospel recording, also on a wax cylinder, was

"I Remember Calvary."

"I remember how my Saviour died for me
On the rugged cross on dark mount Calvary.
I remember how he died,
How he bowed his head and died
I remember dark Calvary."

The Stoneman family were a big success in the sixties with their own weekly T.V. show which, along with all the other bluegrass and mountain music they sang, always featured gospel. With Pop Stoneman setting a pacy rhythm on the autoharp and the rest of the family keeping pace on a mixture of guitar, dobro, mandolin and banjo, and also filling in on the backing vocals, they rattled off songs like the perennial favourite *"Where the Soul Never Dies."*

"My life will end in death asleep
Where the soul never dies.
There everlasting joy I'll reap
Where the soul never dies

"No sad farewell.
No tear dimmed eyes.
Where all is love
And the soul never dies."

TRANSFORMATION

The Stonemans were always religious, but after personal tragedy one member of the group, Donna, the mandolin player turned to Jesus and was born again. She has bid farewell to the bright lights and big money of the country concert circuit and now spends her time travelling over the country, visiting churches large and small, to spread the good news and to bring hope of better days with songs like A.P. Carter's *"Will the Circle be Unbroken."*

"I was standing by my window
On one cold and windy day
When I saw the hearse come rolling
For to carry my mother away.

"Will the circle be unbroken
By and by Lord, by and by.
There's a better home awaiting
In the sky Lord, in the sky.

"I said to the undertaker
Undertaker, please drive slow.
For this lady you are carrying
Lord, I hate to see her go

"Oh I followed close behind her
Proud to hold up and be brave
But I could not hide my sorrow
When they laid her in the grave.

"I went back home, the home was lonesome,
As my mother she was gone.
All my brothers and sisters crying,
But our home so sad and lone.

"Will the circle be unbroken
By and by Lord, by and by.
There's a better home awaiting
In the sky Lord, in the sky."

HYPOCRASY

Donna Stoneman says that at first she didn't like gospel. It meant you had to stand still and that didn't suit the lady who was known for her lively stage performances. She was also put off by some of the people who posed as full time gospel singers.

"I loved what the songs said but I met too many gospel singers that wasn't living it. Then, all of a sudden I turned on to it and now I love it."

A special part of Miss Stoneman's ministry is directed at younger listeners. With her cute little, mandolin pickin', hillbilly puppet perched on her knee she sings simple songs that appeal directly to the children.

"Satan has fooled you,
Thoroughly confused you.
When it comes to lying he's slick.
But God's word is true.
It'll prove to you
God is not dead, He aint even sick!"

BORN AGAIN?

In today's country music scene there's a whole flood of singers who claim, not only gospel roots, but the branches too. *"Born again,"* is a term that's bandied about by all sorts of people but I believe there's a fair number of country singers who've got a real hold of salvation in the New Testament sense of the word. As long as that's the case there'll always be people around to keep alive the traditions and faith of those Appalachian mountain pioneers of generations ago.

"In this modern day we're livin' in
It's hard to understand.
So many names upon the door
Of buildings made by man.
Jesus said "I am the door,"
By me ye enter in."
The only way to heaven is
Forgiveness of sin.

"Have you got modern day religion
Or old time salvation,
You know, the kind that makes you
want to shout?
This modern day religion
Could be 'most anything.
But salvation is what it's all about.

"They'll tell you so many don'ts
You won't know what to do.
They make you look just like a saint
When they get through with you.
Unless you have salvation,
God's love within your heart,
The name you wear won't mean a thing
From God you shall depart.

"Have you got modern day religion
  Or old time salvation,
You know, the kind that makes you
  want to shout?
  This modern day religion
Could be 'most anything.
  But salvation is what it's all about.
("Modern Day Religion." Emma Smith)

ten

An Appalachian Pioneer

On a plateau, in the foothills of the Blue Ridge mountains, where two or three Indian trails crossed, a trading post was founded. Years later it grew into a village, and then a small town.

It's still a small town; only a few thousand souls live there. I don't know why because it's one of the most beautiful spots I've ever visited. Its people are friendly and hospitable. Crime is virtually unknown there, people still don't lock their doors at night, and life is lived at a steady, but easy pace.

Clayton, north Georgia is my kind of town. Surrounded by those beautiful Blue Ridge mountains and densely wooded forests, it seems nearer to heaven than almost any other place I've been to.

Clayton doesn't have a theatre, or a cinema. There's no MacDonalds, no Burger King, none of the other well known fast food outlets. But that doesn't matter. A drive of only a few miles will bring you to half a dozen places that'll serve you a breakfast of crispy bacon, eggs any style, grits and muffin.

ILLUSTRIOUS ANCESTRY

Into this sleepy little town of Clayton, some thirty years ago, there came an unusual man - a pioneer of sorts. His smiling eyes, kindly face, soft spoken, deep, deep bass voice, with its southern drawl and built in intermittent laugh, makes him a man you love to be in the company of.

I said that Caroll Lee, for that's his name, was a pioneer of sorts. Well he is, a pioneer with a proud heritage.

"I have been asked all my life if I was related to the confederate general Robert E. Lee. For a long time I couldn't answer the question but when I got out of radio and started to research my family I discovered that the surname Lee went back to Shropshire, in England. Two historians say that my immigrant ancestor, Hugh Lee, and Robert E. Lee's immigrant ancestor, Richard Henry Lee were brothers. So although I'm not in direct lineage I come from the same stock."

An illustrious ancestry and a heritage almost any American from the southern states would be proud of.

Robert E. Lee was, of course, the great confederate army leader in the civil war that threatened to tear the Unites States apart. The Confederates were against Abraham Lincoln and his Union army which was backed by all the power and wealth of the industrial north. As such, they were branded rebels, a term that to this day I get the feeling they take a sneaking pride in. Certainly, Carroll Lee makes no secret of his ancestry. And in a way its funny that there's a hint of rebellion in other areas of his ancestry too.

"We go back to Scotland also. Hugh MacDonald came to the colonies somewhere around 1745 to 1750. He was at the battle of Culloden, in 1745. The highlanders were making a march on London to try to take the crown back for Charles, that's Bonnie Prince Charlie. They were met a short distance from London by an army that out numbered them three to one; were repelled and forced back to the highlands.

"However, the prisoners were taken and put on prison ships and sent to the colonies. I have an account of the prisoners that details which ones were on which ship, who the master of the ship was, their age, their condition and their description. In there I found Hugh MacDonald, aged thirteen, who could have been a bugle boy or whatever. Anyway he was shipped over to the colonies. He came into Bermuda, in the Bahamas at first, and then later migrated over to South Carolina where he wound up in Craven county. So I feel sure that I've got the right Hugh MacDonald."

MAN OF VISION

Coming from such an illustrious fighting ancestry it's no wonder that Carroll Lee is a man of such vision and determination. It was that determination that took him from an obscure Carolina town to the top of his chosen profession - broadcasting.

Caroll Lee's career in radio broadcasting has been long and varied. He has just retired from almost thirty years of radio station ownership and management, but before that he worked in stations all over the south land. Yet he says he got into the business, more or less, by accident.

"I was in the entertainment business prior to that. I travelled with a group and naturally, in those days, it was radio instead of television that was the big thing. We didn't have big concert halls or anything of that nature. We went to school houses, auditoriums, court houses, wherever people met in the community and we performed on stage, entertaining the folks for two or three hours, every night, except Sunday, throughout the year."

It was a tough circuit, singing and playing to the locals in small towns and hamlets all across the country, night after night. However, Carroll Lee was both cutting his teeth and serving his apprenticeship.

"We gave them music and singing. I played the big bass violin, sometimes called a dog house bass, because they didn't have electric bass back in those days. We played everything from Beethoven to Bluegrass, and everything else in between."

THE ARISTROCRATIC PIGS

Like many another group back in those days, Carroll and his colleagues were sponsored by a commercial company. That being so the stage name they used was almost mandatory.

"We performed for a company that packed processed pork sausage and meat. That, naturally, brings to mind the animal from which pork is taken, the pig. We were the "Aristocratic Pigs!"

Carroll Lee travelled all over the Carolinas with the *"Aristocratic Pigs,"* playing at all sorts of doos. Usually, the crowds were quite small, at least by today's standards. But now and again they hit the big time.

"These days you have concerts where you're playing to fifty thousand people possibly. Back then if you played to three or four hundred you were elated, you had a big crowd. I do recall that we had two nights running, even back then, where we played to eight thousand people. One of those was in

Columbia, South Carolina, the other was in Greenville, South Carolina. That was tremendous."

RADIO CALLS

At the same time as following this heavy schedule of concerts and shows all over the country, Carroll and his buddies did the odd spot on some of the local, small radio stations. That was to be his ticket to a whole new world and way of life.

"After the travelling I came back home to where I grew up, in Anderson, South Carolina. A friend of mine and myself did two radio programmes every day. We did fifteen minutes in the morning and another fifteen minutes in the afternoon. We sang to the accompaniment of two guitars. At vacation time my friend went away on holiday and I did the programmes myself. I did all the music, all the singing and the continuity between the programmes too.

"Well it turned out that the people who ran the station were kinda taken with my delivery of the commercials so they asked me if I'd join the staff as an announcer. I accepted immdiately because I was open for something after having just come off the road. I wanted to settle down and do something that didn't force me to be on the road every night."

That first stint in radio, back in 1942, lasted only a few weeks but it whetted Carroll Lee's appetite for more. In those early days, if you worked in a radio station, you had to be capable of doing everything; announcements, news, adverts, music programmes, a bit of engineering and sometimes even the unexpected.

EMERGENCY!

"This gentleman who owned the station had a series of manufacturing plants and he travelled from one place to another in his own aeroplane. He had been travelling in a very small capacity plane and after 1945 he decided to step it up a little bit and not be up there so long, so he converted an A26 bomber to travel in.

"I was working in his station one day and he was flying to the town where the station was located. It so happened that he had left the airport without clearance. It was overcast and there was a mountain peak that was about four

miles distant from our radio tower. All of a sudden the phone rings and the gentleman on the other end said 'Mr Laturno has departed this airport without clearance and he has had just about enough time to reach your point. If there is anything you can do to get him down we'd appreciate it.'

"Well, as you know, you don't have direct communication with anyone on the radio. However, I had heard this plane lumbering back and forth so I knew he had arrived in the area. Now this mountain peak stuck up about nine hundred feet above the local terrain and he had to keep dodging that. So I opened the mike and said 'For the benefit of any aircraft flying in this area our ceiling is approximately 200 feet and we will monitor the conditions and if it changes we'll let you know."

Carroll went back to his programme and the music while the boss continued to circle the mountain top looking for a gap in the clouds.

HAPPY LANDING!

"Providentially, I went to the door and looked out toward our tower and there was a break in the cloud cover directly over the tower. So I went back to the mike and broadcast a message to that effect. Well down through that break in the clouds came this lumbering A26, right above our tower, and 200 feet off the ground. As he approached the airstrip he was at an angle and when he saw where he was he realised that he was below the landing strip. So he revved that thing up, pulled it up, winged it over and set it down on the strip without incident. However, when he got close enough to the hangar, so that he could run in there and call me, he told me how grateful he was and that he had just five minutes of fuel left."

Caroll concludes his account with another burst of his infectious chuckle but says nothing about the marvellous, life saving power of radio. You would have thought, given the circumstances, the presence of mind of Carroll Lee at the microphone, and who the boss was, that he would have given his rescuer a tip, at least. In the event he didn't. Perhaps he took the view that Mr. Lee was doing no more than he was being paid to do - talking on the wireless. But Carroll Lee wanted to do more than that. He wanted to own a radio station.

"I worked at a number of stations in about a sixty mile radius of this general area and the last station I worked for was over in South Carolina. I wanted to get into radio for myself and it so happened that the gentleman for whom I

worked had a construction permit to build a radio station here in Clayton. I told him that I'd like to have an interest in a radio station and that I was looking around for the right opportunity.

"So he said that if I stayed with him we would activate this construction permit and build the station in Clayton. He said I could manage it for the necessary years and then at the end of that time he would sell it to me at a reasonable price.

"Well we first operated that station in 1961 and at the end of three years it became ours."

PIONEER RADIO

Setting up a radio station, especially back in those pioneering days, wasn't easy. Broadcasting in the U.S.A. was controlled, still is controlled, by the F.C.C., the Federal Communications Commission. Their rules were tight.

Technology was a lot different too. Recordings were made on sixteen inch diameter vinyl discs, which could be used only once and then had to be discarded. Furthermore, the equipment, being big and cumbersome, couldn't easily be taken on location.

"After that the first thing we had was a wire recorder. You had this tiny wire that passed over the magnetic head as you recorded and the electrical charges were on the wire. Then when it passed over the reproduction head you heard what was there. The thing about it was that you had no protection on whether the thing was going to break or not. Should it break, you tied a knot in the wire and when you played it back there would be a big blip as it went across the reproduction head.

"Then in the forties there arrived the first recorders using magnetic tape. These were reel to reel machines and you had the capability of recording up to an hour on one reel of tape. So that served the purpose for many, many years."

TELEVISION

With the new tape recorders Carroll Lee and his radio colleagues felt they were working on the very edge of a technological revolution. Indeed they were, for television was just around the corner and that would introduce further big changes.

"Radio folks, they were ringing their hands at the advent of T.V. But it was the best thing that ever happened because it rejuvenated radio to the point that some stations tripled their advertising revenue. The simple reason was that T.V. cost the merchants so much that not everybody could afford it. This made the merchants who could not participate in T.V. advertising realise that they had to reach the public.. So they came back to radio en mass. It was only the big fellows that could afford the T.V. So it had quite the opposite effect than they had expected. T.V. really was a blessing in disguise. So radio blossomed there for a long time and is still doing well."

Running a radio station isn't as easy as you might think, and not any easier in America. Income depends on advertising, and that's only successful if people, in sizeable numbers, listen to the programmes. About ten years after Carroll Lee took over his radio station, the big country music explosion hit the U.S.A. Up till then they had played a mixture of all types of music, but when country hit in a big way, they had to go with the flow.

"We had other things on the radio besides the music. We were very active in the community. We provided public affairs programmes where we talked about politics and school bond issues; that sort of thing. My wife conducted a weekly public affairs programme where people from the community and dignities from the state would come in and be interviewed in person. The governor's wife came once and we had one of our prominent senators from the state of Georgia who came a number of times to be interviewed. So we tried to keep the community informed on issues that were in front of us and available to us. But the main stay was music. It paid the bills."

Carroll Lee is one of those characters they tell us are no more. I could have listened to his stories of the early days of radio for much longer. But when the coffee pot was empty and the hands of the mantle clock approached midnight it was time to bid him good-bye. It's unlikely we'll ever meet again but my visit to Appalachia was greatly enriched by the hours we spent together.

FAREWELL TO THE APPALACHIANS!

My farewell to Carroll Lee coincided with my farewell to Clayton and the Blue Ridge mountains. Hopefully, I'll return one day to savour more of it's splendid delights. Till then I suppose I'll just go on singing the words of that old Laurel and Hardy song.

"In the Blue Ridge mountains of Virginia
On the trail of the lonesome pine.
In the pale moonshine our hearts entwine.
Where she carved her name
And I carved mine.
O June, just like the mountains, I'm blue,
Like the pine, I am lonesome for you.
In the Blue Ridge mountains of Virginia
On the trail of the lonesome pine."